Basketball's
STACK OFFENSE

Previous books by the author

The Flex-Continuity Basketball Offense
Complete Book of Zone Game Basketball
Basketball's Pro-Set Playbook
Pressure Game Basketball
Seven Championship-Tested Basketball Offenses
Tempo-Control Basketball
Successful Team Techniques in Basketball
Coaches' Guide to Basketball's 1-4 Offense

Basketball's
STACK OFFENSE

Harry L. "Mike" Harkins

Parker Publishing Company, Inc.

West Nyack, New York

Library of Congress Cataloging in Publication Data

Harkins, Harry L.
  Basketball's stack offense.

  Includes index.
  1. Basketball—Offense.   2. Basketball—Coaching.
I. Title.
GV889.H332   1984   796.32'32   84-3194

ISBN 0-13-069451-7

Printed in the United States of America

Dedication

This book is dedicated to my wife, Grace, who, along with being the love of my life, has been a working partner in the books I have written. Without her meticulous efforts on the diagrams and hours spent typing, they might never have been completed.

How This Book
Will Help You

The stack maneuver was originally conceived to be a quick-hitting power move. It permitted a coach to take advantage of the abilities of a strong inside man and a jump-shooting forward. Since its inception, it has evolved and, now along with being a power move, it is used: to initiate set plays against pressure and help man-to-man defenses, to be interjected into continuities by way of looping cuts around downscreens, and even as a functional option against zone defenses. In the latter case, the screener makes the downscreen to pin the zone inside as the cutter pops out and away from the defense, for a possible jump shot.

The use of stack plays received its biggest impetus with Ed Jucker's great book *Power Basketball*. The stack play has since become one of basketball's standard maneuvers, alongside such moves as: the give and go, the screen and roll, the pass and screen-away, backdoor plays, and others.

The stack play is usually run with the jump shooter ((3) in Diagram I-1) lined up inside the power player (5). Their line is usually parallel to the free-throw lane line and outside it.

(5) initiates the action by moving down to screen (3)'s defender. (3) steps in the lane and then moves out to a position as high as the free-throw line extended. (3) cuts close to (5). (5), after setting the screen, back-pivots away from X3. The result is very often a defensive switch that could lead to an easy jump shot for (3), or a post-up mismatch, with (5) being guarded by the much smaller X3. See Diagrams I-2 and I-3.

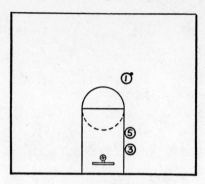

Diagram I-1

In Diagrams I-2 and I-3, if a shot was not forthcoming, further play action would follow.

This book examines the possibilities of the stack maneuver in several ways.

Chapters One, Two, and Three concern the single stack offense. They examine it in the context of a novel, tilted 2-1-2 single stack offense.

Chapter One presents the tilted 2-1-2 single stack offense against a man-to-man defense. This chapter offers a suggested offense as such.

Chapter Two includes auxiliary plays that may be added or substituted for plays in Chapter One.

Chapter Three shows how the tilted 2-1-2 single stack offense may be run against zone defenses.

Chapters Four, Five, and Six examine the double stack offense.

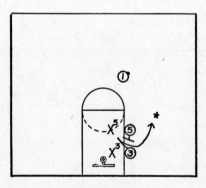

Diagram I-2

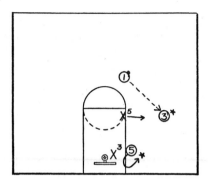

Diagram I-3

Chapter Four offers a group of outstanding double stack plays versus man-to-man defenses.

Chapter Five offers double stack alternatives in the form of auxiliary plays.

Chapter Six shows how the double stack man-to-man plays may be adapted to facilitate their use against zone defenses.

Chapters Seven, Eight, and Nine deal with stack motion plays. They show how a smaller and/or more mobile team may utilize the stack maneuver in the context of motion.

Chapter Seven has some very functional motion play against man-to-man defenses.

Chapter Eight provides auxiliary plays that may substitute for, or add to, the ones in Chapter Six.

Chapter Nine shows how motion plays may be run against zone defenses.

Chapter Ten is comprised of special situation plays. Many of them are related to or involve the stack maneuver.

The book concludes with final comments as to the advantage of the stack offense.

This book does not simply describe one stack offense. It is a catalog of stack plays. This abundance of ideas will permit you to select the stack plays, formation, and type of motion that best fit your personnel and overall coaching situation.

Mike Harkins

ACKNOWLEDGMENTS

Grateful appreciation is expressed to the sources of my basketball knowledge, including:

Russ Estey and Mike Krino, my high school coaches.

Russ Beichly and Red Cochrane, my college coaches.

Buck Hyser, who gave me my first coaching job.

And the players who have played on my teams.

A final note of thanks goes to my number-one fans (and granddaughters) Shellee Ann, and Jamee Cameron Harkins.

Contents

SECTION 3. STACK MOTION PLAYS (111)

. . . .

SECTION ONE

The Single Stack Offense

. . . .

ONE

• • • • • • • •

The Single Stack
Tilted 2-1-2 Offense

This chapter describes an offense that "tilts." It features a novel offensive alignment that attacks and overcomes modern "pressure" and "help" defenses. The concept of "tilt" derives from the movement of a player to the high post area and the concomitant positioning of a two-man stack down low, alongside of the free throw lane. The movement of alternating players to the high post area, combined with the simultaneous shifting of the stack from one side of the free throw lane to the other, creates a continuity of "weak side" and "strong side" with a tilted, unbalanced configuration.

PERSONNEL ALIGNMENT

Ideally, the strongside guard ((1) in Diagram 1-1)) should be the team's best ball handler. (2), the offside guard, can be the weaker guard. This might be a place to play a large guard who would improve your defensive and rebounding strength, but lacks great guard skills. The stacking forward (4) should be a strong jump shooter and have the ability to "feed" the post man. (3) in Diagram 1-1 is the offside forward who moves to the high post area. He should have high post skills, especially the ability to charge the boards. (5) is the team's big man who must be a strong one-on-one player, and passer.

From this tilted formation, patterns and plays may be run, with their options, to either the strong side or weak side of the court.

STRONGSIDE AND WEAKSIDE OFFENSES

The strongside offense is a straight-line, pivot-oriented set of plays with many cuts to the basket. Putting (3) in the high post area gives low post man (5) a lot of room to work and confuses the average pressure-and-help team. Passes are also made to (3) from the strongside offense and he is in an ideal position to pass to cutters, or to feed low post man (5). See Diagram 1-2.

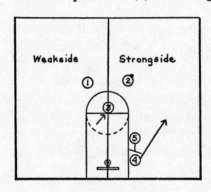

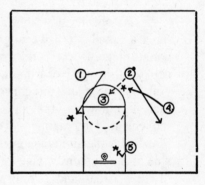

Diagram 1-1   **Diagram 1-2**

The weakside offense has the attribute of being initiated with a dribble entry. See Diagram 1-3.

This, too, foils the plans of the pressure-and-help team by not requiring a penetration pass to start the offense. Strong pressure-help defensive teams are especially tough on the offenses keyed by penetration passes, and can often disrupt them. Once the weakside offense is initiated, it consists of a series of continuous stacking plays designed around a triangle concept.

Post man (5) can tilt the offense toward (3)'s side by posting on that side. When this happens, (3) stacks inside (5) and (4) moves to the high post area. See Diagram 1-4.

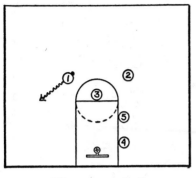 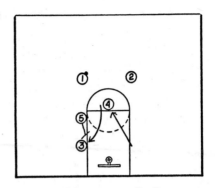

Diagram 1-3   **Diagram 1-4**

From this tilted stack formation, plays are run to either the strong side or weak side of the court.

WEAKSIDE OFFENSE

Play Keys

When the offense is initiated on the side away from the post man, we call this stratagem "weakside plays." The two basic weakside plays both start as guard (1) makes a dribble entry to the cleared wing area. This makes (2) the cutter. He may slash-cut behind forward (3) in the high post area as shown in Diagram 1-5 or over (3) as shown in Diagram 1-6.

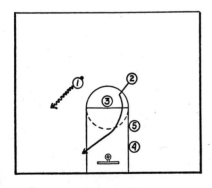 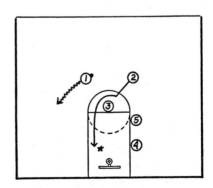

Diagram 1-5   **Diagram 1-6**

Weakside Play #1: Slashcut Play

When (2) slashes behind (3), he continues to the ballside low post area. (3) then steps out and receives a pass from (1). As soon as this happens, (5) downscreens for (4), who pops out for a possible jump shot. After screening, (5) rolls inside. See Diagram 1-7.

(1) also screens down for (2), who pops out looking for a pass from (3). In Diagram 1-8, (3) passes to (2).

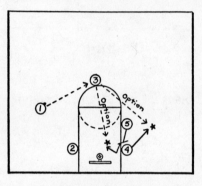

Diagram 1-7   **Diagram 1-8**

(2) may shoot, or look for (5) coming across the low post area off a screen by (1). See Diagram 1-9.

If (5) is not open, (3) screens down for (1), who pops to the head of the key. From there, (2) screens down for (5), (4) screens down for (3), and the inside triangle movement is repeated. See Diagrams 1-10 through 1-13.

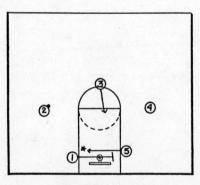

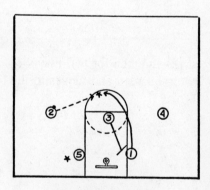

Diagram 1-9   **Diagram 1-10**

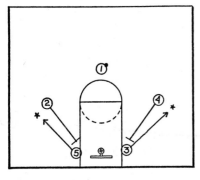

Diagram 1-11   **Diagram 1-12**

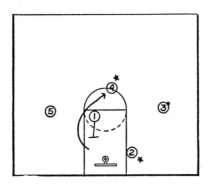

Diagram 1-13

Weakside Play #2: The Overcut

This time, after (1) has made his dribble entry on the weak side, (2) chooses to cut over the post. When this happens, (1) looks quickly at (2) and then for (4). Player (4) uses (2)'s move across the lane as a natural screen and moves to the ballside low post area. See Diagram 1-14.

If neither (2) nor (4) is open, (3) steps out and the inside triangle movement is repeated. See Diagrams 1-15 through 1-17.

(1) and (5) screen down for (4) and (2). See Diagram 1-15.

(3) chooses to pass to (2) and this tells (5) to screen away for (1). See Diagram 1-16.

(3) screens down for (5) who pops out front. See Diagram 1-17.

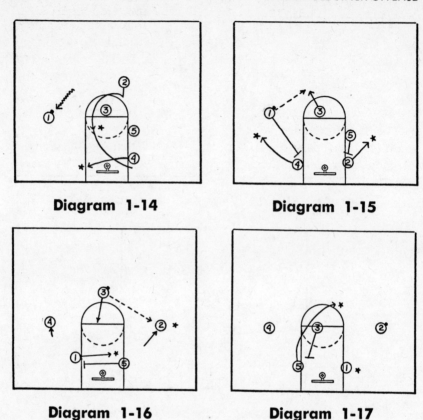

Diagram 1-14   Diagram 1-15

Diagram 1-16   Diagram 1-17

This inside triangle action provides a man moving to the ball off a screen in the low post area. The offside defensive help is disrupted by the downscreen of the man at the apex of the triangle.

Since this weakside offense is initiated with a dribble entry, it makes the guards' jobs much easier. However, after this movement has been run awhile and scouted by the opposition, much pressure will be exerted on (1)'s pass to (3). (3) must learn to step back into his defender and time his cut, as he moves away from him. Since this pass receives so much pressure, a special option is run called "away."

The Away Option

This time, after (1) has made his dribble entry, (2) (knowing that (3) is being pressured) cuts away. See Diagram 1-18.

This tells (3) that a backdoor move is available to him. (3) moves to the head of the key and is pressured by X3. From there, two things must happen simultaneously. As (3) makes his backdoor move, (4) must loop around (5) and to the head of the key. See Diagrams 1-19 and 1-20.

(4)'s move takes away the primary defensive helper, X4, and gives (3) an unmolested lay-up.

If (1) cannot pass to (3), he passes to (4) out front, and the triangle operation is initiated with downscreens on each side of the lane. See Diagram 1-21.

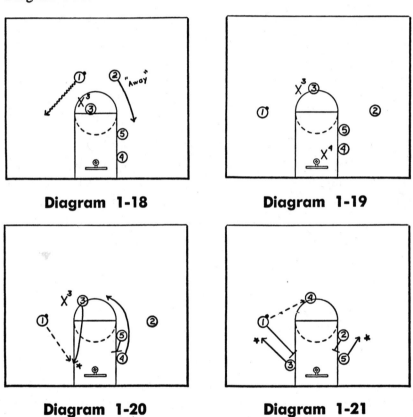

Diagram 1-18   Diagram 1-19

Diagram 1-20   Diagram 1-21

STRONGSIDE OFFENSE

When the offense is initiated on the side of the low post man, it is called "strongside offense."

Strongside Play #1: Pass to Low Post

As (2) brings the ball up court, he bounce-passes to low post man (5), who comes to meet the pass. (2) may now (A) screen for (1), or (B) for (4), who popped out of a downscreen set by (5), and cut to a wing position.

When option (A) happens, the screen for (1) is not a set screen. Rather, it is a moving cut off (3) by (2) that must be utilized by (1). (1) can do this by faking a cut to the basket and using both (2) and (3) on his cut to the ball. See Diagram 1-22.

These cuts provide several fine options. (2) may be open for a lay-up on his cut off (3). (1) may get a short jump shot on his cut off (2) and (3). Also, note that (4), upon not receiving a screen from (2), backdoored his man and could have been open for a jump shot in the corner. (4) also might have been able to take the ball to the basket. (5) hits the open man or makes a one-on-one play. The movement of this play takes away the defensive help on (5) and facilitates his pivot play.

When (2), after passing to low post man (5), chooses to screen for (4), option B, the following movement takes place. (4) fakes his back-door cut and moves to the ball. (1) moves toward the ball, changes direction, and cuts off (3) to the low post area. (2) rolls inside after screening for (4). See Diagram 1-23.

(5) again may hit the open man or make his one-on-one play.

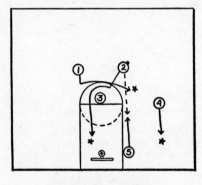
Diagram 1-22

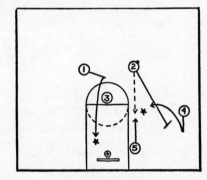
Diagram 1-23

Strongside Play #2: Pass to High Post

When (2), the strongside guard, chooses to pass to (3) in the high post area, he again may (A) screen for guard (1) or (B) for forward (4).

(A) (2) screens for guard (1). After his pass to (3), (2) changes direction and makes a cut over him. (1) makes a change of direction and utilizes (2)'s cut to create a splitting action. At the same time, (4), upon not receiving a screen from (2), cuts to the basket off low post man (5), who sets a definite screen for him. See Diagram 1-24.

Although most of the attention of the defense will be on (2) and (1)'s high post split, the primary option is inside. If (5) can screen (4)'s defender well enough and force a switch, (4) will continue across the lane and take big defender X5 with him. This will leave low post man (5) inside of a smaller defender X4 and should provide a power lay-up shot. See Diagram 1-25.

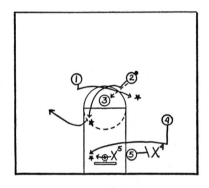

Diagram 1-24

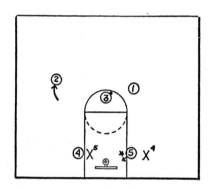

Diagram 1-25

(3) must look for (2) cutting over, (1) on the splitting option, (4) coming over (5)'s screen, and then the primary option is a lob to (5) inside the small defender.

(B) (2) screens for forward (4). This time, after passing to (3) in the high post area, (2) chooses to screen for forward (4). (4) fakes a baseline cut and uses (2)'s screen to move to the ball. (1) starts toward (2), changes direction, and cuts off (3) to the offside lay-up slot. (2), after screening, rolls inside. See Diagram 1-26.

(3) may now pass to (4) coming off (2)'s screen, or look for (1)'s cut to the offside lay-up area. If neither are open, (3) pivots to face (5), who posts up in the low post area. (3) may pass to (5) (see Diagram 1-27), or fake a pass to him and drive to the area vacated by (1). See Diagram 1-28.

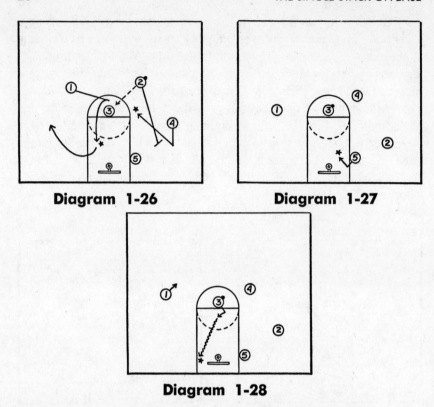

Diagram 1-26   **Diagram 1-27**

Diagram 1-28

Strongside Play #3: Weakside Guard Through Triangle

The triangle play may also be initiated on the strong side. This occurs when strongside guard (2) holds up his hand and calls out "triangle." This tells weakside guard (1) to cut through and either (A) post on the open side (see Diagram 1-29), or (B) swing across the lane (see Diagram 1-30).

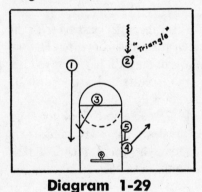

Diagram 1-29

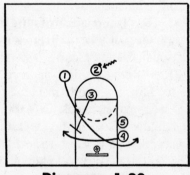

Diagram 1-30

(A) (1) moves to open side: When (1) cuts to the open side, (3) screens down for him and (5) screens down for (4). (1) and (4) then pop out, (2) passes to one of them, and the triangle action is initiated. See Diagrams 1-31 through 1-33.

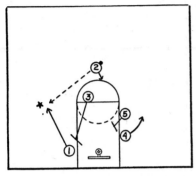

Diagram 1-31

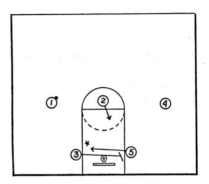

Diagram 1-32

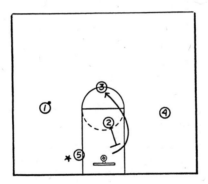

Diagram 1-33

(B) (1) moves across the lane: (1) cuts through, moves across the lane, and this tells (4) to cross the lane. (1) receives a downscreen from (5), (4) receives a downscreen from (3), and the triangle action is initiated. See Diagrams 1-34 and 1-35.

Strongside Play #4: Outside Cut

When guard (2) passes to (4) after he has popped out of (5)'s downscreen, the outside cut play is run. (2) goes outside (4) and continues to the ballside corner. See Diagram 1-36.

From there, forward (4) and guard (2) simply exchange strongside assignments. (4) feeds either the high post (3) or low post and screens to either side, and (2) uses the screen when it is for him and cuts to the basket when it is not. See Diagrams 1-37 through 1-40.

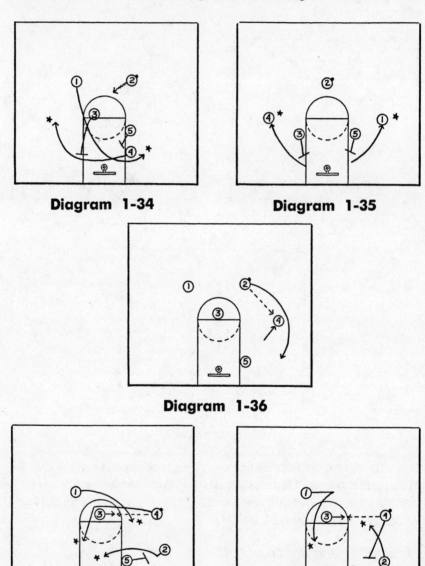

Diagram 1-34

Diagram 1-35

Diagram 1-36

Diagram 1-37

Diagram 1-38

High Post Passes

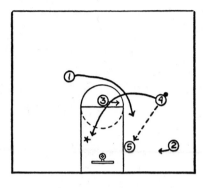

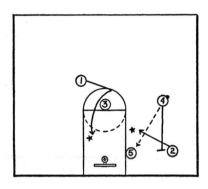

Diagram 1-39   **Diagram 1-40**

Low Post Passes

This offense features a stack power game keyed by guards cutting off the high post man. The power game is accompanied by pivot-oriented set plays that are very difficult to defense. Both phases of the offense are run from a very unorthodox 2-1-2 tilted alignment. This set negates many of the standard man-to-man pressure and help rules and puts the defense in a precarious position.

The offense is easy to teach because, in effect, the weak side is the stack side and the strong side is the split side. This simplicity makes it easy to create repetitive drills that lead to great efficiency in these two basic offensive techniques.

COACHING TIPS—WEAKSIDE OFFENSE

(2)'s Cut Over (3)

This cut, whether over or slash, is a scoring option. (2) must be taught to make a jab step before making his cut. This sets up (3)'s natural screen and gives (1) time to pick up his dribble and make a well-timed pass to (2). A two-handed overhead pass works well in this situation. See Diagram 1-41.

(3)'s Pop-Out Reception and a Pass to Stackers

(3) must learn to back into his defender and move away from him. He should provide (1) with a target using his hand farthest away from defender X3. Upon receiving the ball, he must pivot on his inside foot

to avoid a traveling call. His first option is to look inside to post man (5). (5)'s screen will occur a split second before (1)'s, and this will give (3) enough time to get the ball to (5) as (1) and the ballside post man exchange. Passing inside to (5) is a winning option. It gives your strong inside man (5) a pivot play close to the basket. This leads to many easy baskets and causes the defense to commit many fouls. (3) must feed him away from X5. See Diagram 1-42.

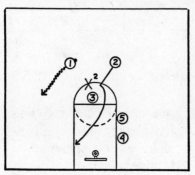

Diagram 1-41

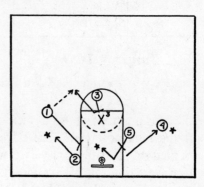

Diagram 1-42

(3)'s Pass to the Wing

When (3) passes to (5)'s wing man, there is a chance (5) may be open inside. (5) should hesitate and attempt to pin his fronting or ¾ playing defender X5 before pivoting inside. See Diagram 1-43.

If the pass is not made because X5 fought and assumed good defensive position, (5) screens away for (1). See Diagram 1-44.

This maneuver should not take more than the allowed three seconds in the lane.

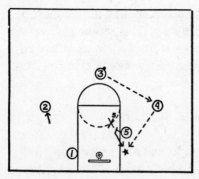

Diagram 1-43

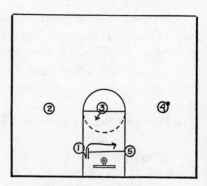

Diagram 1-44

Taking the Pressure Off (3)

The dangerous pass of the weakside offense is the pass from (1) to (3). The backdoor play for (3) ("away") should be run early in the game and immediately following an interception of th(s pass. (2) calls the play with his cut away.

COACHING TIPS—STRONGSIDE OFFENSE

The strongside offense is based on a splitting action after a pass to the post. Again, the secret is a jab step by (4), the man for whom the screen by (2) is intended. For example, in Diagram 1-45, (2) bounce-passes to (5) in the post and chooses to screen for forward (4). By tak-

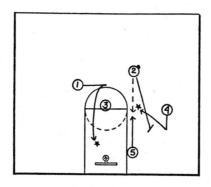

Diagram 1-45

ing a jab step away from the screen, it gives (2) a chance to get there and prevents (2) from being charged with a moving screen foul.

In the diagram above, please note that (1) made a jab step before cutting over (3) for his backdoor move.

(5) then must have good peripheral vision and see the open man. He can best do this by assuming a low stance off a jump stop and receiving the ball in an all-purpose position. These cuts and the subsequent passes must be drilled over and over until they become second nature and (5) can both see and anticipate the location of the cutters.

These same ideas apply to the entire strongside offense.

TWO

. . . .

Auxiliary Plays
for the Tilted 2-1-2
Single Stack Offense

Auxiliary plays are maneuvers that may be added to your offensive repertoire to meet special situations, take advantage of your team's specific strengths, exploit a weakness of a certain team, or simply to give your offense more depth. Also found in this chapter are pressure reliever plays that equip a team to cope with today's pressure and help man-to-man defenses.

WEAKSIDE OFFENSE

Post down Option ((2) Slash Cuts)

(1) makes his dribble entry and (2) cuts off high post man (3). Then high post man (3), instead of popping to the head of the key, screens down for (2) who pops back out front. See Diagrams 2-1 and 2-2.

From there, (1) passes to (2), (4) pops out of (5)'s downscreen, (2) passes to either wing man, and the triangle options are run. See Diagrams 2-3 through 2-5.

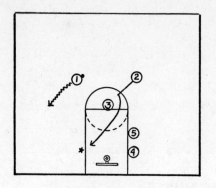

Diagram 2-1

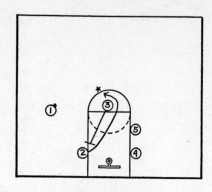

Diagram 2-2

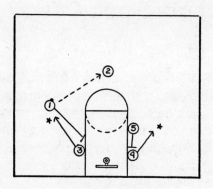

Diagram 2-3

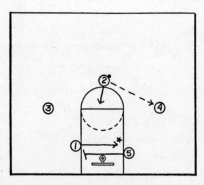

Diagram 2-4

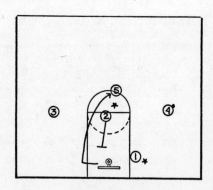

Diagram 2-5

Post down Option ((2) Over Cut)

In Diagram 2-6, (2) cuts over top of (3), looks for a pass from (1), and then loops around the double screen of (5) and (4). This tells (4) to cut to the ballside, low post area.

(3) then screens down for (4), who cuts to the head of the key. See Diagram 2-7.

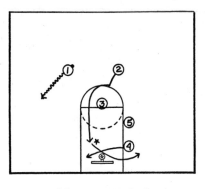

Diagram 2-6   **Diagram 2-7**

(1) then passes to (4) at the point, (4) passes to (3), and the triangle options may be run. See Diagrams 2-8 through 2-10.

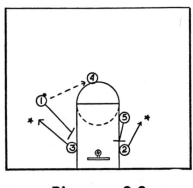

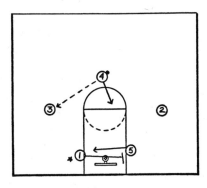

Diagram 2-8   **Diagram 2-9**

The Number 4 Play

This play is run in a last second situation to take advantage of the skills of your best player ((4)). (1) makes his penetration dribble, (2) cuts through and across the lane, and (3) moves to the head of the key to receive a pass from (1). See Diagram 2-11.

(4) may now go either way. (A) He can use (5)'s downscreen and pop out to the wing for a possible pass from (3). See Diagram 2-12.

In this case, if (3) cannot get the ball to (4), he returns it to (1). This tells (4) to cut off the double screen of (5) and (2). See Diagram 2-13.

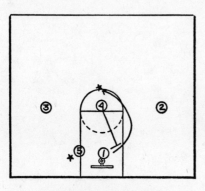

Diagram 2-10

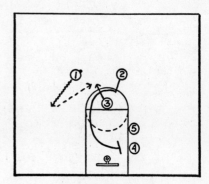

Diagram 2-11

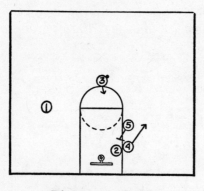

Diagram 2-12

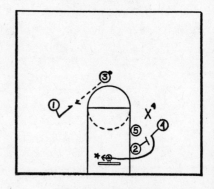

Diagram 2-13

(B) He can use (2) and cut across the lane for a possible pass from (3). See Diagram 2-14.

If (4) is not open, (1) screens down for him and he cuts to the wing area for a pass from (3). See Diagram 2-15.

If (4) was not open, (3) could have passed to (2) moving out of (5)'s downscreen.

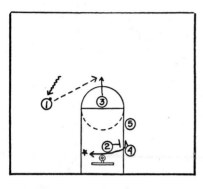

Diagram 2-14

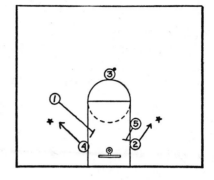

Diagram 2-15

Screen-and-Roll Play

(1) makes his dribble entry and maintains the dribble. (2) slash-cuts off (3) and clears to the ballside corner. See Diagram 2-16.

(3) then steps out to screen for (1), who dribbles off him for a screen-and-roll play. On the offside, (5) screens down for (4), who pops out front. See Diagram 2-17.

(1) may shoot, pass to (3) rolling, or look for (4) or (5).

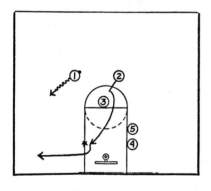

Diagram 2-16

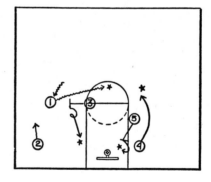

Diagram 2-17

No-Penetration Play

Some teams, after scouting this offense, attempt to force (1) to the inside and disallow any penetration. When this happens, (3) must cut to the wing and receive a pass from (1). (1) then screens away for (2), who may initiate a play. See Diagrams 2-18 through 2-20.

In effect, (3) and (1) have changed assignments.

Guard-to-Guard Pressure Reliever

Another method of initiating the offense when (1) is being denied the dribble entry is to have (2) bring the ball into the front court. He then passes to (1) and cuts to the ballside wing. See Diagram 2-21.

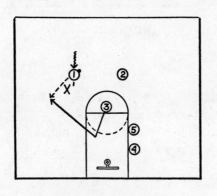

Diagram 2-18

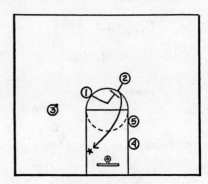

Diagram 2-19

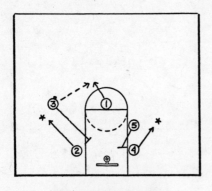

Diagram 2-20

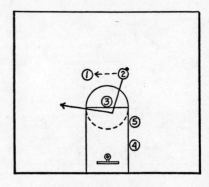

Diagram 2-21

(1) then passes to (2) and slashes (or cuts over) (3). From there, either play may be run. See Diagrams 2-22 and 2-23.

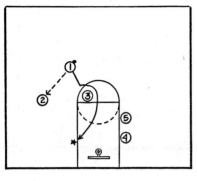

Diagram 2-22

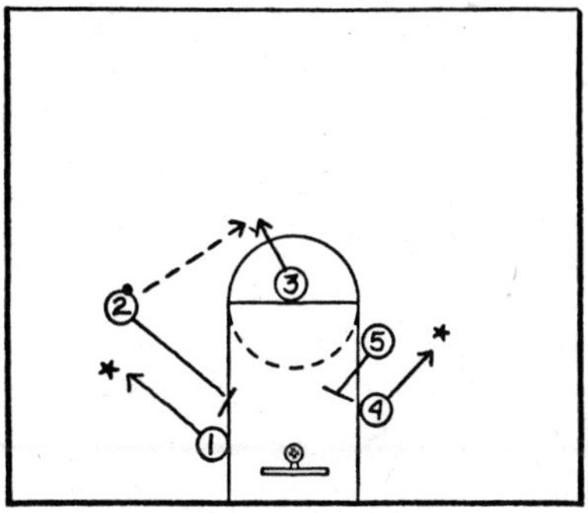

Diagram 2-23

The Guard Hook Play

This play begins as (1) (in Diagram 2-24) brings the ball up the court and (2) cuts down the lane. This time, (2) chooses to set a definite screen on the top man in the stack, (5). (5) uses the screen and cuts across the lane toward (1), who has now dribbled to the sideline.

If (5) is not open, (2) hooks back to the high post area off a screen set by (3). See Diagram 2-25.

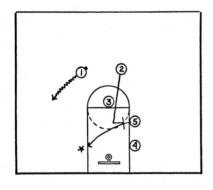

Diagram 2-24

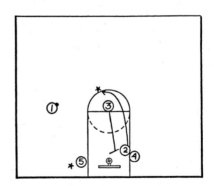

Diagram 2-25

(1) then passes to (2), who may shoot or look for (3) looping around (4)'s downscreen, or (5) coming off (1)'s downscreen. See Diagram 2-26.

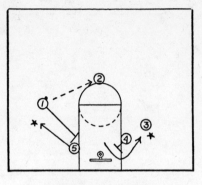

Diagram 2-26

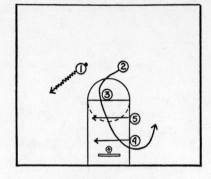

Diagram 2-27

The Double Across Play

(1) makes his dribble entry, (2) cuts over (3), and moves across the lane. This time, both (5) and (4) use (2)'s cut as a natural screen as they move across the lane. See Diagram 2-27.

(2) continues his cut all the way back to the point. (4) then moves toward (1) and loops over a double screen by (5) and (3) (who move down from the high post). (4) then watches for a possible lob pass from (1). See Diagram 2-28.

If (4) is not open, (1) passes to (2) and cuts across the lane below (3) and (4). (2) can pass to (1) or to (3), popping out of (5)'s downscreen. See Diagram 2-29.

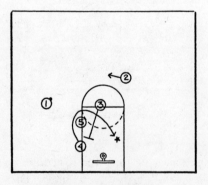

Diagram 2-28

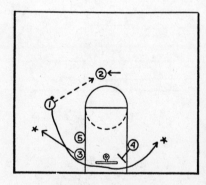

Diagram 2-29

The Guard Loop Play

As (1) makes the dribble entry, (2) cuts over (3) and continues across the lane. (4) calls the guard loop by not cutting off (2). This tells (2) to "loop" around (5) and (4) and back to the ballside, low post area. See Diagram 2-30.

(3) then steps out and the triangle movement is resumed. See Diagrams 2-31, 2-32, and 2-33.

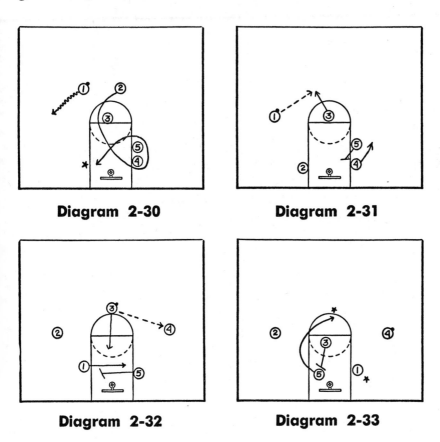

Diagram 2-30   **Diagram 2-31**

Diagram 2-32   **Diagram 2-33**

The Screen-Away and Offside Lob Play

(1) has made his dribble entry and (2) his slash cut to the ballside, low post area. (3) pops out and receives a pass from (1). See Diagram 2-34.

After (1) passes to (3), (4) pops out of (5)'s downscreen, but (2) clears to the corner. See Diagram 2-35.

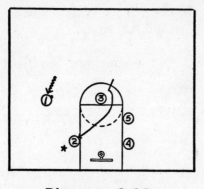

Diagram 2-34   **Diagram 2-35**

(3) looks for (4) and then passes to (2) coming off (1)'s screen in the corner. By now, (4)'s man has fought over (5)'s downscreen and is tight on (4). (5) then steps out and blindscreens X4 as (4) cuts to the ballside, low post area. See Diagram 2-36.

After (4) has cut by, (5) moves up and blindscreens X3 as (3) moves to the basket for a possible lob pass from (1). See Diagram 2-37.

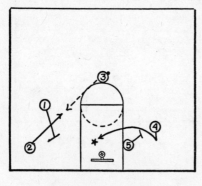

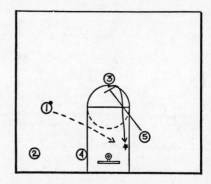

Diagram 2-36   **Diagram 2-37**

This screen-away and lob option may be run at any time during the triangle motion.

STRONGSIDE OFFENSE

Outside Cut Corner Play

After (2) has passed to (4) and cut outside to the corner, (4) cannot get the ball to a post man. When this happens, he passes to (2) in the corner and cuts through. This tells (5) to step out and work a screen-and-roll play with (2). See Diagrams 2-38 and 2-39.

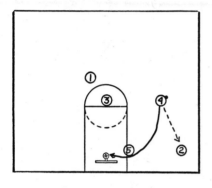
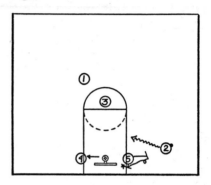

Diagram 2-38   **Diagram 2-39**

Outside Cut to Flex

After (2) has passed to (4) and made his outside cut to the corner, a flex pattern may be run. (4) may pass to (3). This keys (5) to step out and screen for (2), who cuts to the basket for the first flex option. See Diagram 2-40.

Note that (1) cleared to the offside wing area. (4) then screens down for (5) and the flex is in operation. See Diagram 2-41.

UCLA Type Outside Cut Lob Play

This time, (2) passes to (4), cuts outside, and receives the ball back from him. (4) then cuts over a definite screen set by (3) and looks for a lob pass from (2). See Diagram 2-42.

If (4) is not open, (2) dribbles off (3). (5) clears to facilitate (3)'s roll, and (1) screens down for (4). See Diagram 2-43.

The same play can be initiated with a dribble entry on the strongside. This time, (2) dribbles at (4) and clears him over (3) for the

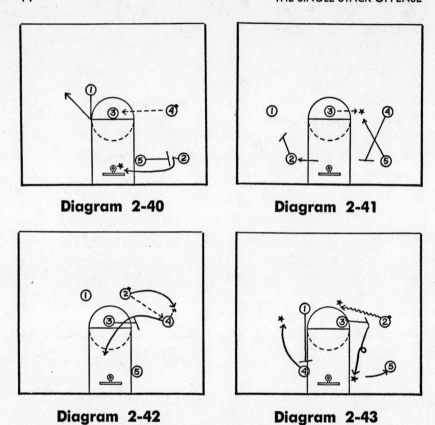

Diagram 2-40   **Diagram 2-41**

Diagram 2-42   **Diagram 2-43**

possible lob. (2) must maintain his dribble and initiate the second phase of the play. See Diagrams 2-44 and 2-45.

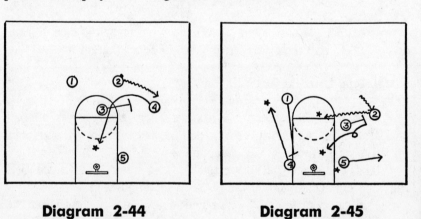

Diagram 2-44   **Diagram 2-45**

The Backdoor Stack Play

In Diagram 2-46, guard (2) passes to high post man (3), and (1) backdoors his defender. (2) changes direction and becomes the second man through.

If (1) is not open, he may:

(A) Stop in the low post area and receive a screen from (2), who is moving toward him. At the same time, (4) pops out of (5)'s downscreen. See Diagram 2-47.

or

(B) Cut across the lane and around (4) and (5). This tells (4) to cross the lane and utilize (2)'s downscreen. See Diagrams 2-48 and 2-49.

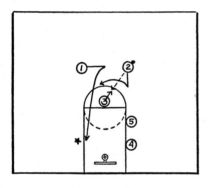

Diagram 2-46

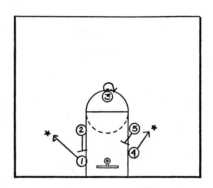

Diagram 2-47

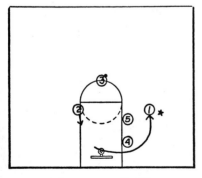

Diagram 2-48

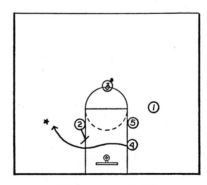

Diagram 2-49

PRESSURE RELIEVERS

Pressure relievers are plays necessitated by today's pressure-and-help defenses. They allow pattern teams to counter the overplay on the ballside and/or remove the help from the offside. Following are plays that anticipate defensive strategies and take advantage of them.

Weakside Pressure Relievers

Post Backdoor Corner Play

(1) makes his dribble entry and (2) cuts through. (3) then steps out, but is overplayed and cannot receive a pass from (1). See Diagram 2-50.

Seeing this, (2) moves to the corner. If (1) is being pressured, he may pass to (2). (3) then backdoors X3 and looks for a pass from (1) or (2). See Diagram 2-51.

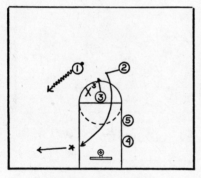 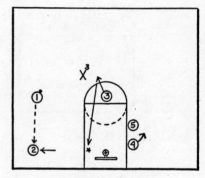

Diagram 2-50   **Diagram 2-51**

(4) then moves to the point off a downscreen from (5). If (3) is not open, the ball is moved back out to (4), who reverses it to (3), looping around (5). See Diagrams 2-52 and 2-53.

From there, the team is back in the triangle rotation. See Diagrams 2-53 and 2-54.

Second Option

At the time (2) cleared to the corner, he also had the option of clearing across the lane. When this occurs, (3) backdoors and (4)

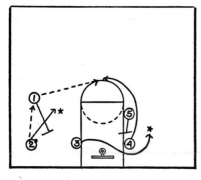

Diagram 2-52

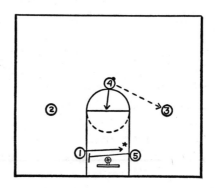

Diagram 2-53

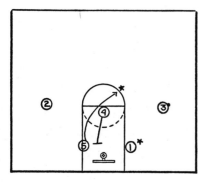

Diagram 2-54

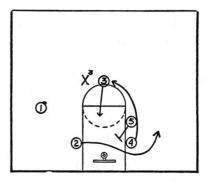

Diagram 2-55

moves to the point. If (3) is not open, (1) passes to (4) and the offense continues. See Diagrams 2-55 and 2-56.

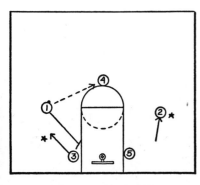

Diagram 2-56

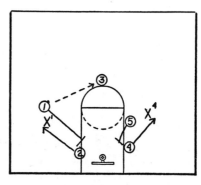

Diagram 2-57

Point Dribble Chase

At times, (3) pops to the front, receives the ball, but cannot pass to the wing men. See Diagram 2-57.

When this happens, (3) dribbles at a wing man ((2) in Diagram 2-58) and causes a perimeter rotation with (4) cutting to the point and (2) clearing to the far wing area.

(3) then passes to (4) at the point and both he and (2) screen down for the man in their respective low post areas. See Diagram 2-59.

From there, the basic inside triangle rotation is run.

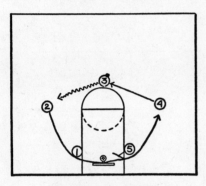

Diagram 2-58

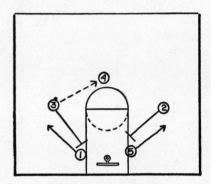

Diagram 2-59

Dribble Wing Loop

The dribble chase may also be run with a wing loop. When (3) makes his dribble chase move at (2), (2) may loop down around (1) and to the point. See Diagram 2-60.

(2) would then receive a pass from (3) and the wings would downscreen to start the inside triangle rotation. See Diagram 2-61.

Double Backdoor

Again, (3) cannot pass to the wing area. Seeing this, both post men break toward the ball and (3) passes to one of them ((2) in Diagram 2-62). (3) looks for (1) on his backdoor cut.

If (1) does not get the ball, he clears to the far wing area. (3) makes a change of direction and gets the ball back from (2), who rolls

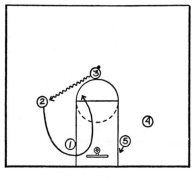

Diagram 2-60

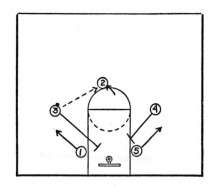

Diagram 2-61

to a low post position. On the offside, (5) screens for (4) moving to the point. See Diagram 2-63.

From there, (3) passes to (4), and the inside triangle rotation is initiated. See Diagrams 2-64 and 2-65.

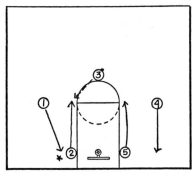

Diagram 2-62

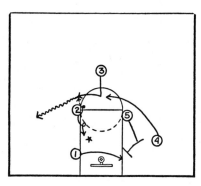

Diagram 2-63

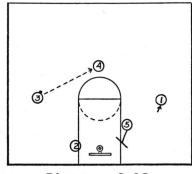

Diagram 2-64

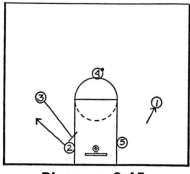

Diagram 2-65

THREE

. . . .

The Tilted
Single Stack Offense
Versus Zones

The tilted 2-1-2 single stack offense may be adapted for use against zone defenses. Following are some of the plays that, with the necessary adjustments, are a strong zone offense. Closing the chapter are some suggestions that will allow you to develop a comprehensive zone plan.

WEAKSIDE PLAYS

Guard Slash Play

When (1) makes his dribble entry, it converts the offense from a two-man front to a one-man front. Then (2) cuts through and (3) steps out to the head of the key and (4) pops out. Each of these changes causes an adjustment in the perimeter of the zone. This is especially true against match-up or adjusting zones which key on the front of the zone offense. See Diagrams 3-1 through 3-4.

(1) then passes out to (3) and downscreens for (2). See

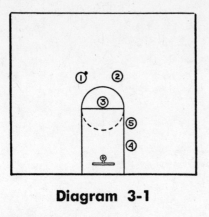

Diagram 3-1

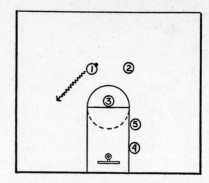
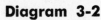

Diagram 3-2

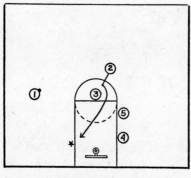

Diagram 3-3

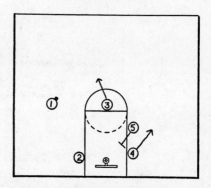

Diagram 3-4

Diagram 3-5. His screen, plus (4)'s pop-out from (5)'s downscreen may elongate the zone and make it porous, or it may trap the zone players inside. (3) is a tall player at the point and he now must read the defense. He may pass to (2) or (4) at a wing position or get the ball inside to (1) or (5). He ((3)) chooses to pass to (4). See Diagram 3-6.

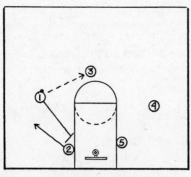

Diagram 3-5

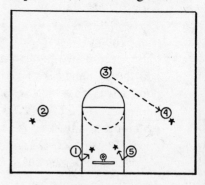

Diagram 3-6

The Triangle Option

Against man-to-man defenses, (5) would screen away for (1) on (3)'s pass to (4). (3) would then screen down for (5) who would cut to the head of the key.

Against zones, a slight adjustment is made. (1) cuts to the high post area on the ball side and three options are then possible: (A) A high post to low post pass play, (B) a low post to high post play, and (C) a clearout play by the low post man (5).

(A) The high post to low post: (4) passes to (1) in the high post, and (1) then passes to (5) inside the zone. See Diagram 3-7.

(B) The low post to high post: This time, (4) passes to (5) in the low post and (1) breaks down, hoping to find a hole in the zone and receive a pass from (5) for a power lay-up. See Diagram 3-8.

(C) The clearout: This is keyed by (4) with a dribble. (5) then clears across the lane and (1) slides down, hoping to get a pass from (4). See Diagram 3-9.

If (1) is not open, (3) exchanges with (5). See Diagram 3-10.

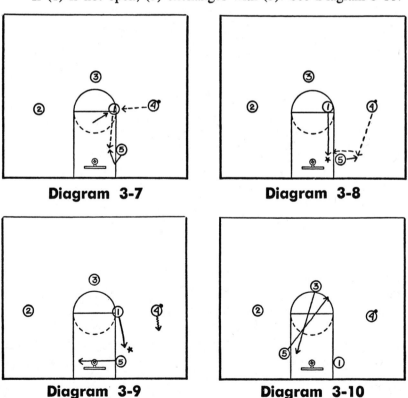

Diagram 3-7   Diagram 3-8

Diagram 3-9   Diagram 3-10

This exchange by (5) and (3) usually has no real function, but it is part of the man-to-man offense and it makes it easier to relate the zone and man-to-man options.

(4) then passes to (5), and the sequence may be repeated. See Diagrams 3-11 through 3-13.

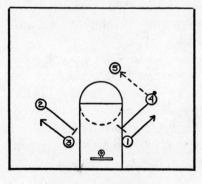

Diagram 3-11

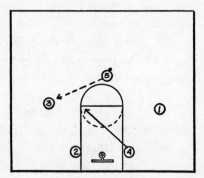

Diagram 3-12

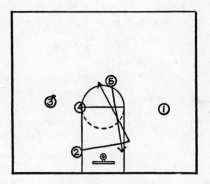

Diagram 3-13

Guard Overcut Play

When guard (2) chooses to cut over (3) after (1)'s dribble entry, it again forces the zone to make front perimeter adjustments. (2) continues down across the lane and around (4) and (5)'s double screen. Against zones, (4) holds his position until (2) gets around him and the ball is reversed to him by way of (3). See Diagrams 3-14 and 3-15.

The double screen by (5) and (4) very often traps the zone inside and provides an unmolested shot for (2).

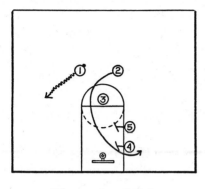

Diagram 3-14   **Diagram 3-15**

If (2) receives a pass and is not open, he dribbles and this keys (4) to clear across the lane, (5) to slide down, (3) and (4) to exchange, and, from there, the play continues as per the guard slash play. See Diagrams 3-16 through 3-18.

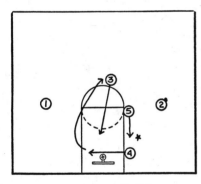

Diagram 3-16

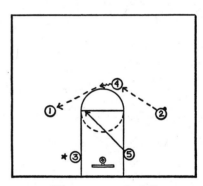

Diagram 3-17

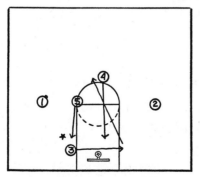

Diagram 3-18

PRESSURE RELIEVERS

The Away Play with "Mouse" Slides

(1) makes his dribble entry and (2) moves to the wing away from the ball to key the "away" play. (3) fakes a cut to the point and cuts to the basket, looking for the ball. At the same time, (4) moves to the point. See Diagram 3-19.

(1) can pass to (3) or (4). When the pass is made to (4), both (1) and (2) dip down inside their respective post men and then pop out (mouse moves). See Diagram 3-20.

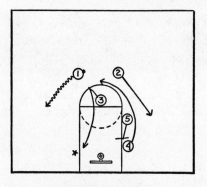   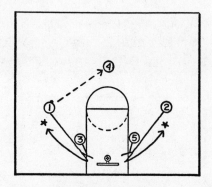

Diagram 3-19   **Diagram 3-20**

(4) then passes to either side ((1) in Diagram 3-21) and the inside triangle move is run.

The advantage to this play is that the three biggest players comprise the inside triangle at all times because of the mouse slides and the fact that (2) cut away to key the play. The fact that the apex of the triangle is always occupied by a tall man is also a plus. This enables the point man to see over the defense and make quick two-hand overhead passes to either wing, or inside to a post man. See Diagram 3-22.

The wide wings tend to spread the zone and facilitate the passes to the post.

The Corner Post Backdoor Play

In Chapter Two (Pressure Relievers), a play very much like the "away play" is shown. It has one further zone attribute that is worth

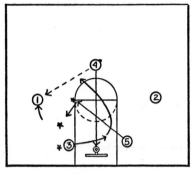

Diagram 3-21

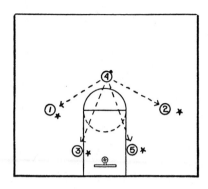

Diagram 3-22

mentioning. (1) has made his dribble entry, and, unlike the "away" play, (2) has cut through to the ballside post area. Versus man-to-man, (3)'s backdoor cut is keyed by (2) clearing to the ballside corner. See Diagram 3-23.

(2) then cuts to the corner. This keys (3) to cut through and replace (2) in the ballside post area. He should look for the ball on this cut. At the same time, (4) swings to the point. See Diagram 3-24.

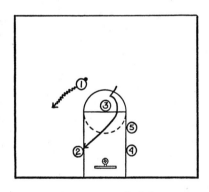

Diagram 3-23

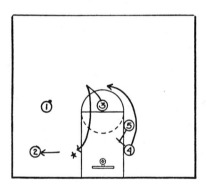

Diagram 3-24

This overload is utilized with (2), (1), (4), and (3) passing the ball until (1) decides to do away with it. He does this by passing to (4) and cutting through to the other wing area. See Diagram 3-25.

(2) replaces (1) at the wing and the inside triangle is run. See Diagrams 3-26 and 3-27.

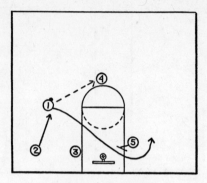

Diagram 3-25

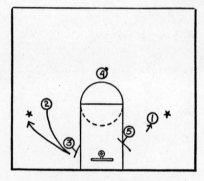

Diagram 3-26

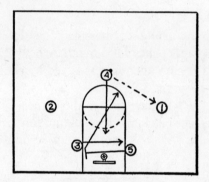

Diagram 3-27

Dribble Chase

Another man-to-man pressure reliever that is functional versus zones takes place at the time the point man must pass to one of the wing men popping out from downscreens. In Diagram 3-28, (3) cannot get the ball to (2) popping out, so he dribbles toward him. This clears (2), and he may:

(A) Overload

Clear to the ballside corner. The ball is then moved around to utilize the triangle formed by (3), (2), and (4), who replaced (3) at the point.

(3) can do away with the overload by passing to (4) and cutting through to the offside wing. (2) would then replace (3) at the wing and the inside triangle would continue. See Diagram 3-29.

Diagram 3-28   **Diagram 3-29**

B. Overshift

Clear to the offside wing. When this happens, (3) quickly reverses the ball back to himself by way of (4). (5) can help (3) get open by screening the zone. See Diagram 3-30.

From there, the inside triangle is resumed.

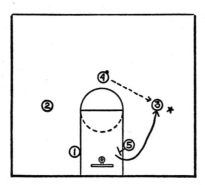

Diagram 3-30

STRONGSIDE PLAYS

The strongside man-to-man offense is very pivot-oriented. Against zone defenses, the post-to-post pass must be emphasized.

Pass to High Post

Against zones when (3) receives the pass from (2), he looks first for (5) inside the zone and then for the perimeter movement.

In Diagram 3-31, (2) passes to (3) and screens for (4) as (1) backdoors.

(2) and (4)'s crossing movement does little versus zones. (3) must first look inside for (5), then for (1), whose backdoor cut took him to the offside wing area.

In Diagram 3-32, (2) passes to (3) and screens for (1) as (4) backdoors to the corner. Again, (2)'s crossing movement with (1) has little function versus zones. (3) looks inside for (5) and then to the weakside wing (2).

If, on either of the plays, nothing opens up, the ball is returned to the perimeter.

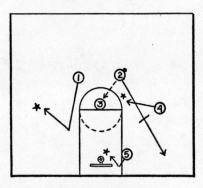   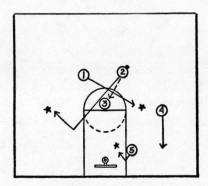

Diagram 3-31   **Diagram 3-32**

Pass to Low Post

The pass from (2) to the post man (5) is not easy to make against zones. However, some zones can be spread out and then penetrated. As (5) receives the pass from (2), he looks first for (3) cutting to the basket. If (3) is not open, (5) checks the perimeter and hits the open man.

Diagram 3-33 shows this play when (2) passes to (5) and screens for (4) as (1) backdoors.

Diagram 3-34 shows this play when (2) passes to (5) and screens for (1).

In either of these situations, the zone may collapse on (5) and leave the onside wing man or corner man open. However, it must be made clear that (3)'s cut to the basket is the primary option. The pass to the offside wing is not probable on the pass to low post man (5).

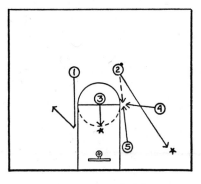

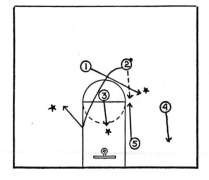

Diagram 3-33   **Diagram 3-34**

In my book, *The Flex-Continuity Basketball Offense*, I stress that a coach should have a four-phased zone plan.

The first phase is previously mentioned—the simple adaptations of man-to-man plays. A coach should also have an uncomplicated zone offense, stress the fundamentals of individual zone offense, and have some tempo-changing devices when things go wrong.

An Uncomplicated Zone Offense

This offense is run from a 1-2-2 set. It begins as point man (1) passes to wing man (2). Offside wing man (3) then breaks to the high post area. See Diagram 3-35.

If (2) passes to (3), he can shoot or look to (4) or (5) inside. If (3) is not open, (4) breaks to the ballside corner, and (2) passes to him and loops to the point as (1) comes to the wing position. See Diagram 3-36.

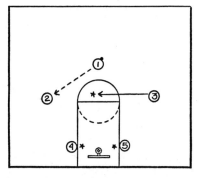

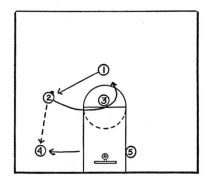

Diagram 3-35   **Diagram 3-36**

(4) then looks for (3) sliding down off (2)'s looping cut. See Diagram 3-37.

If (3) is not open, (4) passes to (1) and the ball is reversed to (5), cutting diagonally to the wing area. (4) and (3) slide over to become the new post men. See Diagrams 3-38 and 3-39.

As shown in Diagram 3-39, (1) then cuts to the middle and the sequence is repeated.

This simple zone play tests the zone in the two most vital areas. It penetrates the middle and then forces it to elongate and cover the corner.

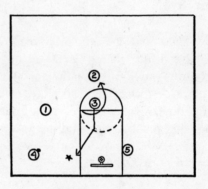

Diagram 3-37

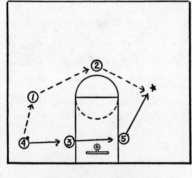

Diagram 3-38

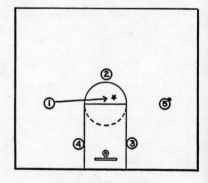

Diagram 3-39

Individual Zone Fundamentals

The players should be taught the following individual fundamentals:

(1) Be alert and attempt to fast break the zone.

(2) If you play between the zone defenders' areas of responsibility, it confuses them.

(3) Move the ball at a planned functional tempo.

(4) Make fakes with the ball, and, when possible, dribble between the defenders.

(5) Throw crosscourt passes. This confuses their planned slides.

(6) Receive the ball in an all-purpose (attack) position which allows you to quickly pass, shoot, or dribble.

(7) To really test the zone, get the ball to the high post area or a corner.

(8) We always go second side. Never initiate the offense on one side and shoot without reversing it to the other (unless the shot is a lay-up).

(9) Study the movement of the defender in your area. If he is slow, take the outside shot; if he is off-balance, penetrate the zone with a dribble.

(10) If you are double-teamed, use the two-hand overhead pass.

(11) We must charge the boards hard when we shoot.

(12) If you find their zone results in a mismatch, take advantage of it.

(13) Know our seasonal zone plan, and execute it.

(14) Know your specific assignment for this game and follow it.

(15) Shoot 50 zone shots each night in practice.

Tempo-Changing Devices

Along with these man-to-man adaptations, individual fundamentals, and zone plays, a team must have tempo-changing devices to be used when its zone plan is not working. They would include:

- A strong running game.
- A zone press.
- A hold-the-ball and pull-them-out plan.
- A zone of their own.

Whatever the method, the idea is to control the game's tempo. Do something different and break the rhythmic zone tempo when it is causing you problems.

This four-phase plan is insurance against the night when your planned zone offense does not work.

· · · · · · · · · ·

SECTION TWO

The Double Stack Offense

· · · · · · · · · · · · · · · · · · ·

FOUR

•   •   •   •   •   •   •   •

The Double Stack
Offense

This double stack offense is a power set that features two big men inside. It is composed of five plays that present the defense with a wide variety of play situations and, in general, keep one or both of the big men inside.

PERSONNEL ALIGNMENT

Probably the key man in this offensive set is the point man ((1) in Diagram 4-1). He must be able to bring the ball up court versus pressure and then initiate the offense. The two wing men ((2) and (3)) must be strong jump shooters and be able to "feed" their respective post man. Big men (4) and (5) must be strong rebounders, tough one-on-one players in the low post areas, and adequate passers. From this formation, the plays are keyed by point man (1) and may be run to either side.

THE DRIBBLE-AWAY PLAY

The play begins as (1) dribbles directly to the sideline without making any penetration. This tells (2) to pop out on that side, the off-side post man (5) to move to the head of the key, and (3) to pop out to the wing area on his side. See Diagram 4-1.

(1) then passes back to the post man and one of two things may happen:

A. Straight Post Up

If (4) can really dominate X4, he posts up and (5) attempts to get the ball to him. This is possible because the cuts of the other players have cleared the post area for the one-on-one play. See Diagram 4-2.

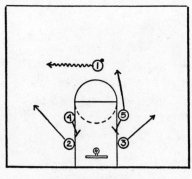

Diagram 4-1

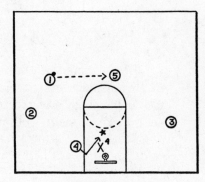

Diagram 4-2

B. Force the Switch

If (4) cannot dominate X4, he can aid his cause when the pass from (1) to (5) is made by stepping out to screen for (2). (2) would then cut to the lane. (2) can go high or low, but the idea is for (4) to force a switch and end up with X2 (a smaller man) guarding him. See Diagrams 4-3 and 4-4, as (2) clears around (3) with big defender X4 guarding him.

If (4) is not open, (5) would pass to (2) and screen away from (4) to exchange with him. See Diagram 4-5.

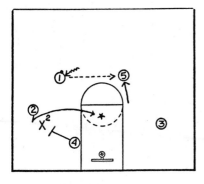

Diagram 4-3

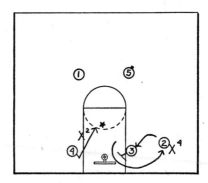

Diagram 4-4

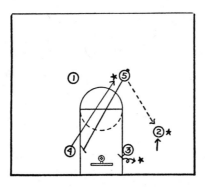

Diagram 4-5

(2), after receiving the ball from (5), could shoot or pass to (4). Once (4) gets the ball, he can pass to (1) and the process is repeated with some different players involved. See Diagrams 4-6 through 4-8.

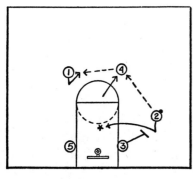

Diagram 4-6

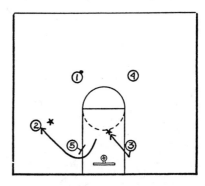

Diagram 4-7

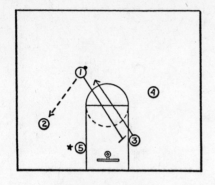

Diagram 4-8   **Diagram 4-9**

The most important thing to remember about this play is that the point man can choose which post man will post up. In the previously described sequence, (1) chose to post up (4). If he desired, he ((1)) could post up (5) by dribbling to his side. See Diagram 4-9.

THE DRIBBLE PENETRATION PLAY

This time, (1) dribbles directly toward a point man ((2) in Diagram 4-10). This move keys (2) to clear out, the onside post man (4) to screen away high, and the offside wing man (3) to pop out to his wing area.

From there, either of two options may be keyed by (2).

(A) (2) may clear low.

(B) (2) may clear high.

(2) Clears Low Option

This option is keyed as (2) clears across the lane and under (5). See Diagram 4-11.

Seeing (2)'s clearing move is low, (3) cuts high using (4)'s screen to cut to the ballside, lay-up area. See Diagram 4-12.

If (3) gets open, (1) passes to him for an easy lay-up shot. If (3) is not open, (4) pops to the head of the key and (1) passes to him. When this happens, (2) moves out of (5)'s downscreen. After (1) passes to (4), he screens down for (3). (4) passes to the open man. See Diagram 4-13.

The conclusion of this play may be run in another way.

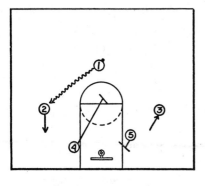

Diagram 4-10

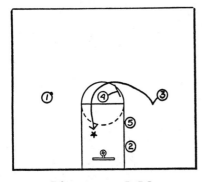

Diagram 4-12

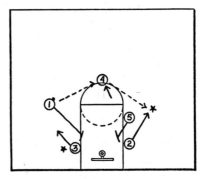

Diagram 4-13

At the point in the previous diagram when (4) can pass to a wing, he chooses to pass to (2), popping out of (5)'s downscreen. (4) then screens for (1), who moves to the point. (2) may now: (A) pass to (5) and split the post with (1) (see Diagram 4-14); (B) pass to (1) to reset

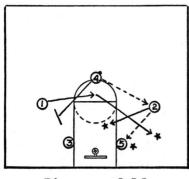

Diagram 4-14

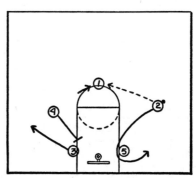

Diagram 4-15

the offense. After receiving the ball, (1) may shoot or dribble at either wing to start the dribble penetration play. (See Diagrams 4-15 and 4-16.)

(2) Clears High Option

(1) has dribbled at (2) and cleared him. This time (2) chooses to clear high. See Diagram 4-17.

Note that (4) again cleared away high and (3) again popped out of (5)'s downscreen.

(3) observes that (2) cleared high, so he cuts low off (5) to the ballside lay-up area to receive the pass from (1). See Diagram 4-18.

If (3) is not open, (1) passes to (2) and screens down for (3). At the same time, (4) screens down for (5). See Diagram 4-19.

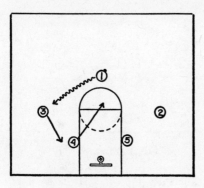

Diagram 4-16

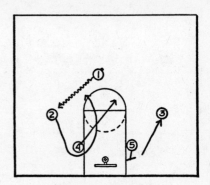

Diagram 4-17

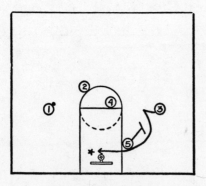

Diagram 4-18

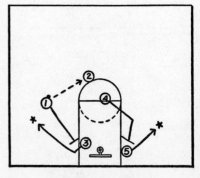

Diagram 4-19

Coaching Point

This play must be run many times in practice with no defenders. Only through repetition will (3) learn to read (2)'s clearing move.

THE CORNER PLAY

This time, (1) brings the ball to (2)'s side, passes to him, and cuts to the ballside corner. This cut tells offside post man (5) to cut to the ballside high post area; (3) to start to the point, backdoor, and look for a possible lob from (2); and ballside post man (4) to post up. See Diagram 4-20.

(2) looks quickly at (3)'s backdoor cut and then passes to (5) in the high post. (5) receives the ball from (2) and looks for (4) posting up inside, and (1) coming off a screen by (2). See Diagram 4-21.

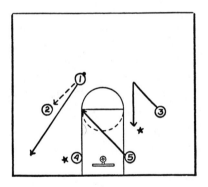

Diagram 4-20

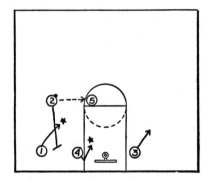

Diagram 4-21

If (5) cannot get the ball to (1) or (4), he fakes a pass to (4) (two-hand overhead) and passes to (3) moving up to the free-throw line extended. (5)'s fake to (4) forced X4 to play him ballside and high. On the pass to (3), (4) does a back pivot and moves ballside for a pass from (3) and an easy lay-up. See Diagram 4-22.

This play has many options, and it too requires discipline and proper execution.

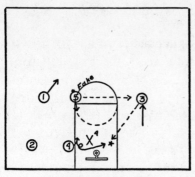

Diagram 4-22

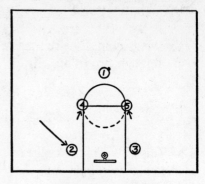

Diagram 4-23

THE DOUBLE HIGH POST PLAY

(1) calls this play by raising his hand as he enters the front court. This tells both post men ((4) and (5)) to move to the high post area. See Diagram 4-23.

(1) can now dribble to either side and utilize the screen set by the post man ((4) or (5)) on that side. In Diagram 4-24, (1) dribbles off post man (5). This tells the inside man on that side, (3), to move across the lane and screen for (2), who moves to the ball.

If (1) or (2) cannot get the shot, (4) and (5) screen down for (3), who moves to the free throw line in a hooking type cut to get a pass from (1) for an unmolested jump shot. See Diagram 4-25.

This is a very fine quick-hitter type play that works well in "last shot" situations.

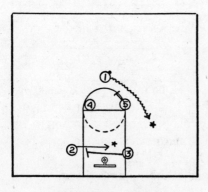

Diagram 4-24

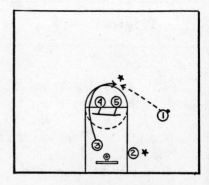

Diagram 4-25

THE BACKDOOR PLAY

The backdoor play is run when point man (1) notices the defense is denying the ball to the players popping out of the stack. In Diagram 4-26, (2) has moved out of (4)'s downscreen and is unable to receive a pass from (1) because of X2's overplay. On the offside, (3) has moved out of (5)'s downscreen stack and he, too, is being overplayed. (1) bounce-passes the ball to post man (4), who comes to meet the pass. The higher (4)'s cut to receive the ball, the better, because it gives (2) room to cut. (2) backdoors X2 and looks for a quick pass from (4) for a lay-up. At the same time, (5) steps out and backscreens for (3), who cuts to the basket. (1) changes direction and clears away from the lane. See Diagrams 4-26 and 4-27.

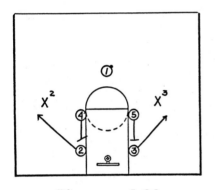

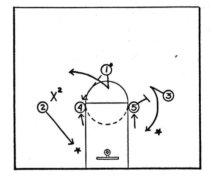

Diagram 4-26   **Diagram 4-27**

(4) can now hit (2) on the backdoor cut or lob to (3) coming off (5)'s screen. If neither is open, (2) stops at the lane and (3) swings around him. See Diagram 4-28.

By now, (4) has pivoted to face the basket. He looks first for (3). If (3) is not open, (2) crosses the lane and hooks around (5), who is moving down the lane. See Diagram 4-29.

(2) can usually get an easy jump shot.

You may feel that five plays are too many. If so, choose any number of these plays for your offense, or, to supplement your present plan, use one or two of these plays.

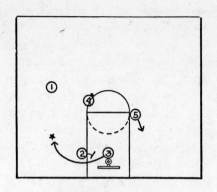

Diagram 4-28

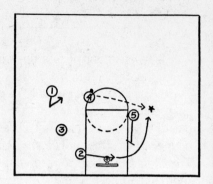

Diagram 4-29

FIVE

. . . .

Auxiliary Plays
for the Double Stack
Offense

The following auxiliary plays may fit your personnel better than the ones in Chapter Four. They also may be used to give the offense more depth or to meet special situations.

THE ENTRY PLAY

One of the problems of running a double stack is to get the wings open for an entry pass after their original pop-out. The answer to this is variety. Following are some suggested methods of varying the original double stack pop-out.

The Basic Down Screen

In Diagram 5-1, (4) and (5) screen down and must get a piece of (2) and (3)'s defenders. They then roll around from any pressure. As for (2) and (3), they follow these rules: (A) if your defender goes below the screener, pop-out at a sharp angle to the free-throw line extended (see (2) in Diagram 5-1); (B) if your defender goes above the screen, flatten your cut and move out toward the corner (see (2) in diagram 5-2).

Some other pop-out options follow.

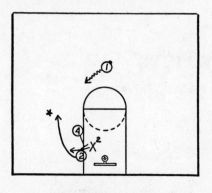

Diagram 5-1   **Diagram 5-2**

Cross

(2) and (3) defenders are playing outside the stack. This tells them to cross and force a difficult defensive switch. See Diagram 5-3.

Big Man Out

When the defense is really tough, the big men, (4) and (5), pop straight out, and, once an entry key is made, they switch jobs with (2) and (3). See Diagram 5-4.

This is also an excellent idea if (4) and (5) are being dominated inside by their defenders.

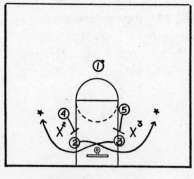
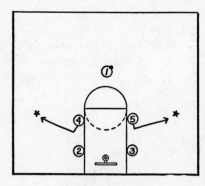

Diagram 5-3   **Diagram 5-4**

The Lead Loop

In Diagram 5-5, (2) is the lead man because (1) has dribbled to his side. He loops all the way around (4) and may be open for a jump shot.

Seeing (2)'s cut, (3) crosses the lane and pops out of a downscreen by (4). (2) clears down and around (5)'s screen. See Diagrams 5-6 and 5-7.

The Backdoor Double Back

This option is more of a scoring play than a move to initiate a play. In Diagram 5-8, (2) and (3) pop out and are denied the pass.

Seeing that (2) and (3) are being overplayed, both (4) and (5) break high and wide. This tells (2) and (3) to backdoor for a possible lob pass. See Diagram 5-9.

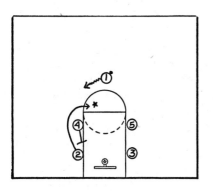

Diagram 5-5

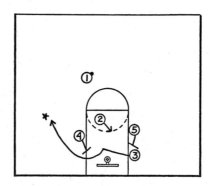

Diagram 5-6

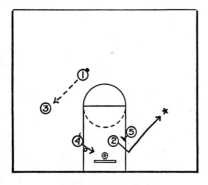

Diagram 5-7

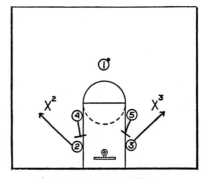

Diagram 5-8

The moves by (4) and (5) may take away the defensive help.

If (2) and (3) are not open, they cross, receive downscreens by (4) and (5), and a new play is started. See Diagram 5-10.

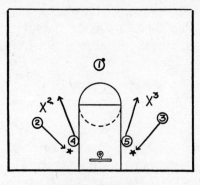

Diagram 5-9

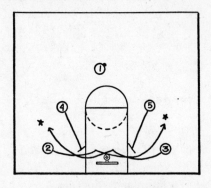

Diagram 5-10

The Late Post Lob

As the ball is brought into the front court by (1), (2) notices that his post man is late getting up court. He then finds him and blindscreens his defender (X4 in Diagram 5-11) for a possible lob pass from (1). Note that (3) popped out to keep the defensive help busy.

If (4) is not open, it is usually because X2 switched. When this happens, (2) pops out to the side, gets a pass from (1), and a play is keyed. See Diagram 5-12.

Once one of these play-initiating moves has been executed, the following plays may be run.

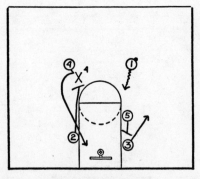

Diagram 5-11

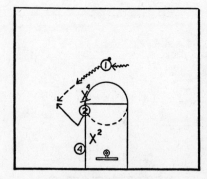

Diagram 5-12

POST BACKDOOR PLAY

When the opposition is doing a good job of denying the passes from the point man to the wings, it is wise to use some variety. An example of this is to have the top man of the stack (post man (5) in Diagram 5-13) cut directly to the sideline, receive the pass from (1), and switch assignments with (3) for whichever play is keyed.

Once this option has been used, the post backdoor play works very well. The defender on (5) usually is a big man who is often unfamiliar with playing pressure perimeter defender. As (5) moves out the second time, X5 will attempt to deny (1)'s entry pass to him. When this occurs, the bottom man of the stack breaks up, receives a bounce pass, and looks for (5), who backdoors his defender. See Diagrams 5–14 and 5-15.

If (5) is not open on the backdoor cut, he cuts across the lane. (1) changes direction and becomes the second man through. See Diagram 5-16.

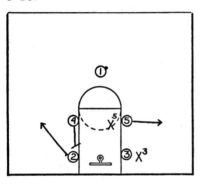

Diagram 5-13

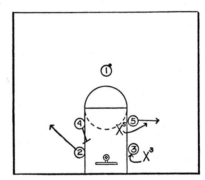

Diagram 5-14

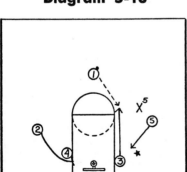

Diagram 5-15

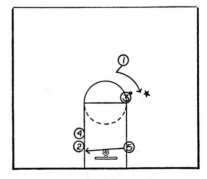

Diagram 5-16

(3) can hand off to (1) or dribble across the lane above the free throw line and pass to (5) behind a double screen set by (4) and (2). See Diagram 5-17.

THE DOUBLE DOWN PLAY

This play begins as (2) and (3) pop out of the downscreens set by (4) and (5). In Diagram 5-18, (1) chooses to pass to (2) and slashes off (4), who moved to the high post area.

The offside post man (5) then moves to the head of the key and receives a pass from (2). Following that pass, both (2) and (4) screen down for (1), who pops out. See Diagram 5-19.

If (1) is not open, (2) clears across the lane and pops out of a downscreen set by (3). See Diagram 5-20.

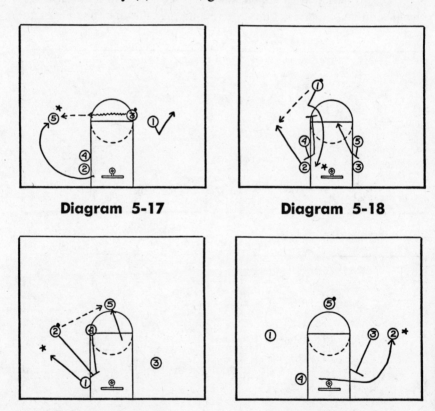

Diagram 5-17   Diagram 5-18

Diagram 5-19   Diagram 5-20

THE LOB OPTIONS FOR THE ONE-ON-ONE POST-UP PLAY

If you have a post man who is obviously stronger than his defender, you can use the one-on-one post-up play mentioned in Chapter 4. This begins with both wing men (2) and (3) coming out of their downscreen. In Diagram 5-21, point man (1) then dribbles toward the side of your dominant post man. The offside post man (5) then cuts to the head of the key.

(1) then passes to (5). If (2) and (3) are good actors and clear wide, this will leave the entire lane open for (4) to play one-on-one with his inferior defender. See Diagram 5-22. This one-on-one post-up idea is also very functional if X5 is a dominant inside defender and you wish to clear him high.

Two lob options may be added to take advantage of the defense. They are: (A) The Point Lob Play, and (B) The Post Lob Play.

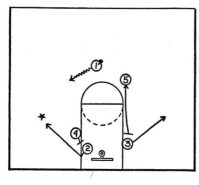

Diagram 5-21

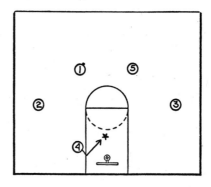

Diagram 5-22

(A) The Point Lob Option

The same basic idea may be used after a point lob option. As (1) comes up court, the offside wing (3) loops around the double screen set by (4) and (2). (5) cuts to the head of the key. See Diagram 5-23.

(1) then passes to (3), moves toward him one step and cuts over (4) and (2) for a possible lob pass. See Diagram 5–24.

If (1) is not open for the lob pass, (3) dribbles toward (5), (2) pops out, and (1) clears wide. See Diagram 5-25.

(3) passes to (5). Note that (5) made a move to get open. Then the one-on-one post-up is run for post man (4). See Diagram 5-26.

The extra play action tends to make it more difficult for the defense to help on (4).

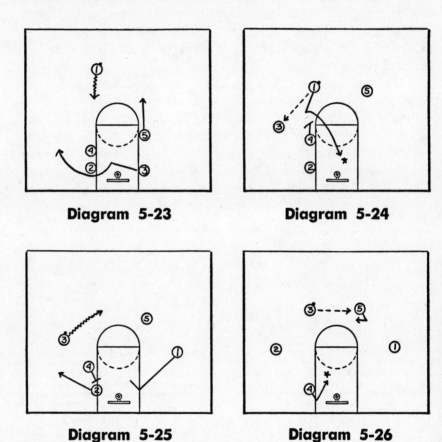

Diagram 5-23   Diagram 5-24

Diagram 5-25   Diagram 5-26

(B) The Post Lob Option

When the defense denies the pass to (5), a lob counter may be added. (3) does not pop out so wide and when (5) is denied, (3) moves up and blindscreens X5. This allows (5) to cut to the basket for a lob pass from (1). See Diagram 5-27.

If the lob to (5) is not open, (1) passes to (3) and (4) posts up. See Diagram 5-28.

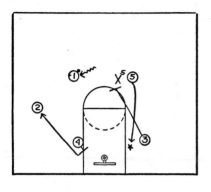

Diagram 5-27

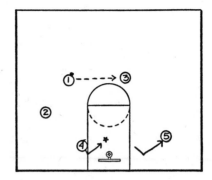

Diagram 5-28

THE PORTLAND PLAY

If more play action is desired, the Portland Trailblazer Play may be run from this key.

This time, (1) dribbles almost to a wing position and (2) does not pop out. (1) passes back to (5) and cuts over (4) and (2). See Diagram 5-29.

If (1) is not open, (2) pops out of (4)'s downscreen. (5) may pass first to (1), cutting over, and then to (2) or (3). When he passes to either (2) or (3), he screens away for the other. Diagram 5-30 shows (5) passing to (2). Diagram 5-31 shows (5) passing to (3).

This play, too, may be used to take the big, dominant defender on (5) away from the basket.

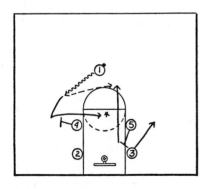

Diagram 5-29

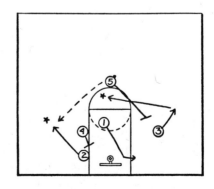

Diagram 5-30

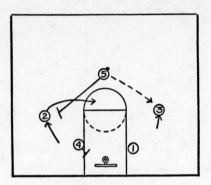

Diagram 5-31

THE DEPAUL PLAY

The DePaul 2-1-2 play may also be run from the double stack formation. This occurs as (1) passes to wing man (2), who popped out of (4)'s downscreen. (1) then cuts diagonally down the lane looking for a lob pass from (2). See Diagram 5-32.

If (1) is not open, (2) passes to (5) in the ballside high post area. (5) reverses the ball to (1), who has looped back and is free-throw line high. See Diagram 5-33.

(2) then cuts off (4) and looks for a pass from (1). See Diagram 5-34.

If (2) is not open, (1) dribbles out front, (2) and (3) move to their wing positions, and (5) moves back to his original position. From there, a new play may be run. See Diagram 5-35.

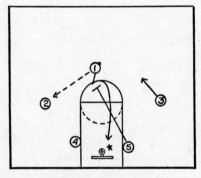

Diagram 5-32

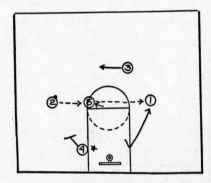

Diagram 5-33

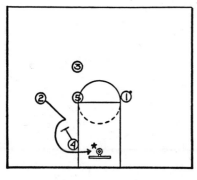

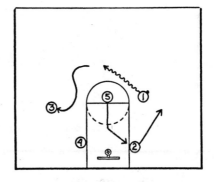

Diagram 5-34   **Diagram 5-35**

THE SCREEN-AND-ROLL PLAY

(1) passes to (2), clears down the lane, and around the double stack of (5) and (3). See Diagram 5-36.

(2) and (4) then work a screen-and-roll play with (2) dribbling off (4). (2) may shoot, hit (4) on the roll, or look for (1) behind the double screen. See Diagram 5-37.

Double-Back Option

(4) can call a special option by moving high as (1) cuts around the double screen. As (1) looks back after clearing, he will see the screen-and-roll did not take place. (1) then doubles back and gets a pass from (2) for a lay-up shot. See Diagrams 5-38 and 5-39.

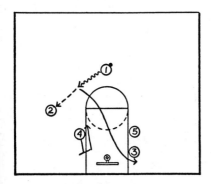

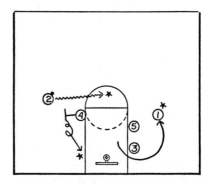

Diagram 5-36   **Diagram 5-37**

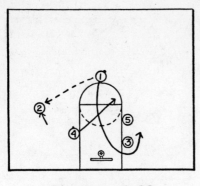

Diagram 5-38

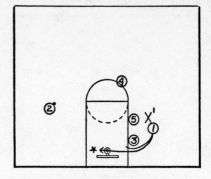

Diagram 5-39

If (1) is not open, (2) passes to (4), who reverses the ball to (3), coming out of (5)'s downscreen. After (2) passes to (4), he downscreens for (1). See Diagram 5-40.

THE PASS AND SCREEN-AWAY POST CLEAR-OUT PLAY

In Diagram 5-41, point man (1) passes to wing man (2) and screens away for wing man (3). This key tells the onside post man (4) to clear to the ballside corner. (3) then has room to cut all the way to the basket.

If (3) is not open, (2) has two options which are: (A) The Reverse Option, or (B) The Post-and-Split Option.

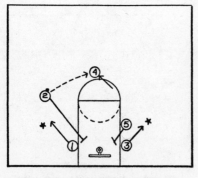

Diagram 5-40

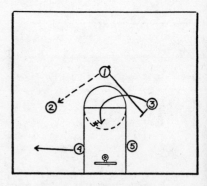

Diagram 5-41

(A) The Reverse Option

The Reverse Option is keyed as (2) passes back to (1) cutting to the ball. The ball is then reversed to (3) coming out of a downscreen by (5). See Diagram 5-42.

(1) would then screen away for (2), (5) would clear to the ballside corner, and this option would be run the second time around. See Diagram 5-43.

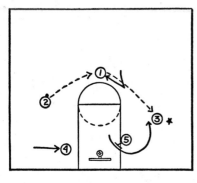

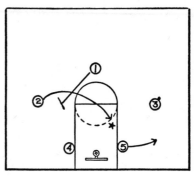

Diagram 5-42   **Diagram 5-43**

(B) The Post-and-Split Option

The post-and-split option is keyed when (2) chooses to pass to the post man in the corner, as to (4) in Diagram 5-44.

This tells the offside post man (5) to use (3)'s cut as a moving screen and move to the ballside low post area. (4) then passes to (5) and splits the post with (2). See Diagram 5-45.

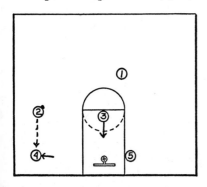

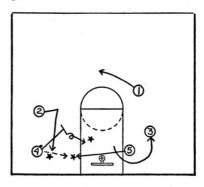

Diagram 5-44   **Diagram 5-45**

AN OUTSIDE CUT PLAY (OR SEQUENCE)

Point man (1) passes to (2) and makes an outside cut. (2) pitches back to him and then does one of two things:

(A) He may run the high screen option, or

(B) He may run the post-up option.

(A) The High Screen Option

After handing back to (1), (2) chooses to cut high and screen for (3), who has moved to the point. This also tells the onside post man (4) to screen away for the offside post man (5). See Diagram 5-46.

(3) then uses (2)'s screen to cut to the ballside lay-up area looking for a pass from (1). See Diagram 5-47.

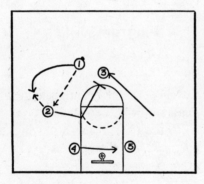

Diagram 5-46

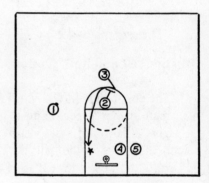

Diagram 5-47

If (3) is not open, (5) uses both (4)'s screen and (3)'s cut to move to the ball for a possible pass from (1). See Diagram 5-48.

If (1) passes to (5), he splits the post with (2). If (1) cannot get the ball to (5), he passes to (2), stepping out to the head of the key. (2) then reverses the ball to (3) coming around 4. See Diagram 5-49.

(3) can shoot or look for (4) inside. If nothing develops, (2) can then make an outside cut and the play is run the second time around. See Diagrams 5-50 and 5-51.

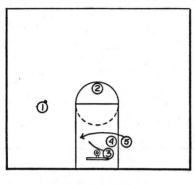

Diagram 5-48

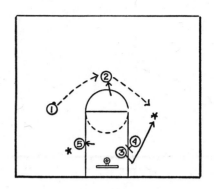

Diagram 5-49

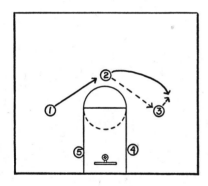

Diagram 5-50

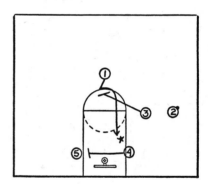

Diagram 5-51

(B) The Post-Up Option

This time, (2), after pitching back to (1), chooses to post up. (4) again clears away to a position that has him stacked under (5). See Diagram 5-52.

If (1) cannot get the ball to (2) in the post, he passes the ball to (3), who looks for (4) popping out of (5)'s downscreen. (1) screens down for (2) to give (3) another passing option. See Diagrams 5-53 and 5-54.

If nothing develops, (4) cuts over (5) as (1) clears under (5), and the team is in position to run a new play. See Diagrams 5-55 and 5-56.

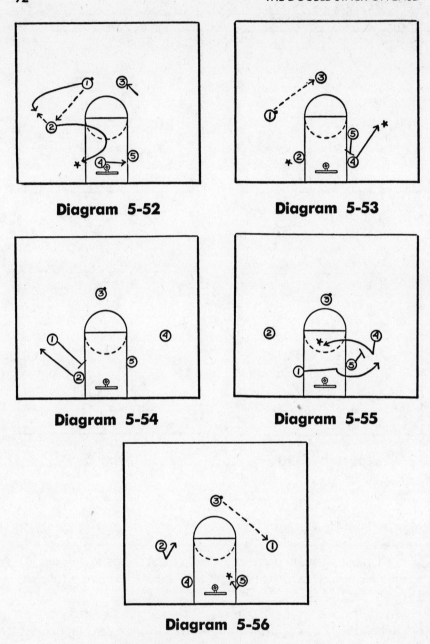

Diagram 5-52

Diagram 5-53

Diagram 5-54

Diagram 5-55

Diagram 5-56

THE PITCHBACK DENIAL PLAY

This time, as (1) passes to (2) and makes an outside cut, X2 fights over and denies the pitchback. (2) then fakes the ball to (1) and dribbles to the middle of the free throw lane and above the free throw line. (1) continues down and around the offside post man. (4) again screens away for (5) and (3) moves to the point. See Diagram 5-57.

(2) may now hand off to (3) cutting to the basket, or look for (1) cutting around (4). See Diagram 5-58.

(5) *must time* his cut and be the third option.

If nothing develops, (2) may pass to either wing and a new play may be run. See Diagram 5-59.

This sequence provides a variety of shot options. However, timing is very important and much practice time must be spent in developing it.

Some other pitchback denial plays follow.

THE WING FAKE PLAY

In Diagram 5-60, wing man (2) pops out of (4)'s downscreen and receives a pass from (1). (1) then makes his outside cut as if to receive

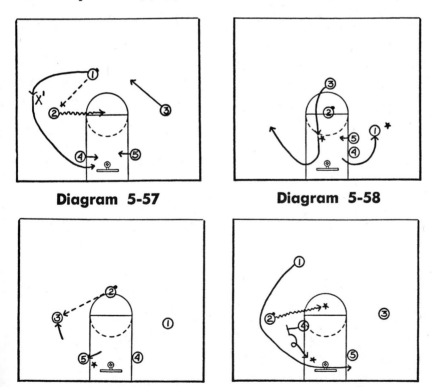

Diagram 5-57   **Diagram 5-58**

Diagram 5-59   **Diagram 5-60**

a return pass from (2). This time, however, (2) fakes the return pass to
(1) and dribbles above (4) and to the high post area. At the same time,
(1) cuts across the lane and (4) rolls to the basket.

(2) may shoot or pass to (4). If neither of these options is open, (3)
moves toward (2), takes a pass from him, and then looks for (1) coming out of (5)'s downscreen. See Diagram 5-61.

This play is very similar to the previous play, but players (1) and
(2) have exchanged assignments.

The Lob Option

A lob option that takes place following the screen-and-roll in either the (A) Outside Cut Screen-and-Roll Play or the (B) Wing Fake
Play, works as follows:

(A) The Outside Cut Screen-and-Roll Play

(1) in Diagram 5-62 has passed to (2), takes an outside cut, and
receives the ball back from (2). (1) then dribbles over post man (4).
This time (4) fakes a roll and moves up to the high post area. The offside wing man (3) cuts above (1) and uses a screen from (4) to get open
for a possible lob pass from (1). (1) may pass to (3) on the lob option or
look for (2) popping out of (5)'s downscreen. See Diagrams 5-62
through 5-64.

(B) The Wing Fake Play

Diagrams 5-65 through 5-67 shows this same lob option being run
from the wing fake play.

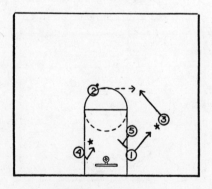

Diagram 5-61

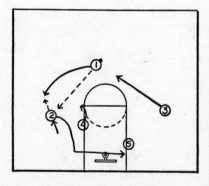

Diagram 5-62

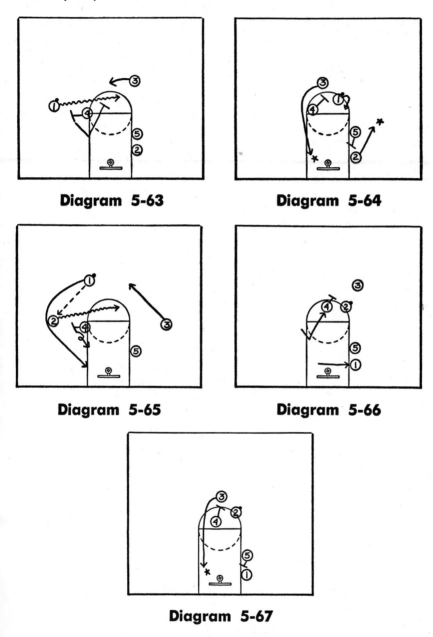

Diagram 5-63

Diagram 5-64

Diagram 5-65

Diagram 5-66

Diagram 5-67

A NOTE OF CAUTION

The dribbler must be very careful as he dribbles by (3). He must protect the ball from X3 and be wary of double teams.

SIX

• • • • • • • •

Set Plays
from the Double Stack
Versus Zone Defenses

The following man-to-man plays may also be used against zone defenses.

THE DRIBBLE AWAY PLAY

In Diagram 6-1, point man (1) is the lane player out front. As he dribbles toward the sideline, offside post man (5) moves out front, and both bottom men in the stack ((2) and (3)) pop out.

This move changes the offense from an odd-man front ((1) alone) to an even-man front ((1) and (5)). (1) then passes to (5), and (2) cuts to the high post area. See Diagram 6-2.

If (5) can get the ball to (2), (2) may turn and shoot, or look inside the zone to (4) or (3). See Diagram 6-3.

If (5) cannot get the ball to (2), (2) loops down and around (3) to the ballside wing area, and (4) pops up to the high post area. See Diagram 6-4.

(5) then has three options. He may: (A) pass to (2) out-

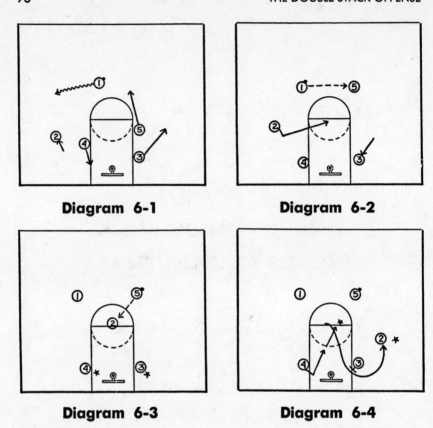

Diagram 6-1   Diagram 6-2

Diagram 6-3   Diagram 6-4

side (3)'s downscreen, or (B) pass to (4) in the middle. When the pass is made to (4), (1) backdoors to the offside free-throw line extended area. (4) may shoot, reverse the ball to (1), or look for (3) inside the zone. See Diagram 6-5. (C) (5)'s third option is to pass to (1). When this happens, the play is run again. (4) slides down to his original position, (2) cuts to the middle, and then down and around (4). (3) then pops high and (5) backdoors to the free-throw line extended. See Diagrams 6-6 through Diagram 6-8.

THE CORNER PLAY

After (2) and (3) have popped out of the downscreen stacks, (1) passes to (2) and calls the corner play by cutting to the corner. This tells the offside post man (5) to cut to the ballside post area, the low

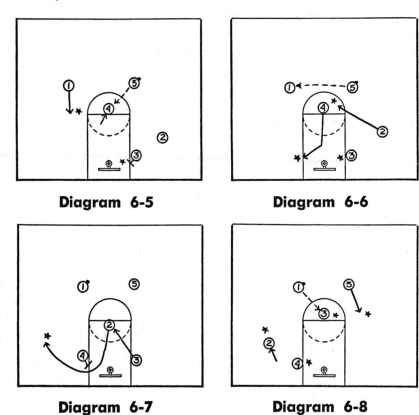

Diagram 6-5   **Diagram 6-6**

Diagram 6-7   **Diagram 6-8**

post man (4) to post up, and the offside wing man (3) to move to the basket. See Diagram 6-9.

(2) then attempts to get the ball to (5). When this is accomplished, (5) looks for (4) inside the zone, then for (1) moving off (2)'s screen that attempts to trap the zone inside. See Diagram 6-10.

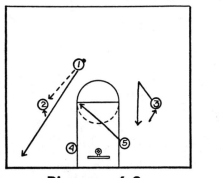

Diagram 6-9

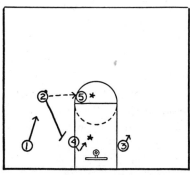

Diagram 6-10

If neither (4) nor (1) are open, (5) reverses the ball to (3), moving up to the free-throw line extended on the offside. When this occurs, (4) comes across the low post area, (5) slides to the offside post area, and (1) continues his cut back to the point. See Diagram 6-11.

If (4) is not open, (3) returns the ball to (1) and the play may be run again. See Diagrams 6-12 through 6-14.

Note: This play may, of course, be run on either side.

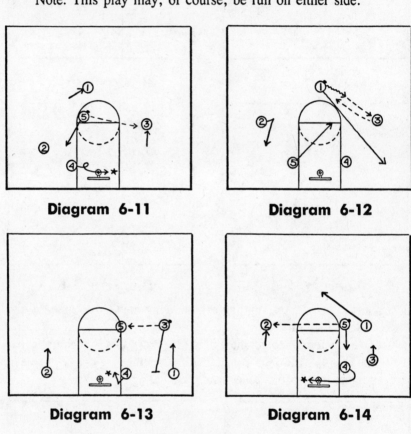

Diagram 6-11   **Diagram 6-12**

Diagram 6-13   **Diagram 6-14**

THE DRIBBLE ENTRY PLAY

Running this play versus zones requires a few timing and cutting adjustments. However, it works very well once these are accomplished. Point man (1) dribbles at a wing man ((2) in Diagram 6-15), and clears him across the lane to form the bottom of a stack with (5). This clearing dribble tells the onside post man (4) to (rather than screen away high as per the man-to-man play) move to the head of the key.

The offside wing man (3) then cuts to the high post area. If he is open, (1) passes to (3), who looks inside the zone to (5), or to (2), who popped out of the stack to a wing position. See Diagram 6-16.

If (1) cannot get the ball to (3), (3) slides down to the ballside low post area and (1) passes to (4), who reverses the ball to (2) popping out of (5)'s downscreen. See Diagram 6-17.

If nothing develops, (1) moves to the point and receives the ball from (2). At the same time, (4) moves down from point to screen for (3), and starts a new play. See Diagram 6-18.

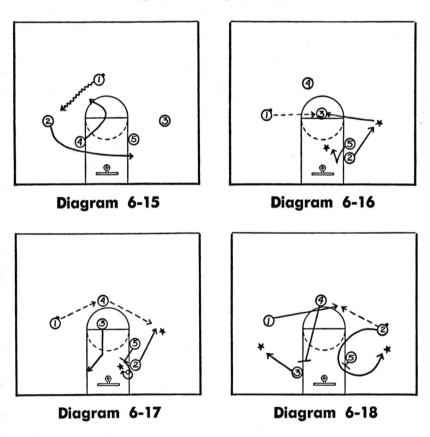

Diagram 6-15   Diagram 6-16

Diagram 6-17   Diagram 6-18

THE PASS AND SCREEN-AWAY PLAY

The pass and screen-away man-to-man play is also a strong zone play.

In Diagram 6-19, point man (1) passes to wing man (2), and screens away for (3). The screen by (1) has little value, but the cut by

(3) is very functional if he makes it free-throw line high. If (2) can pass to (3), he may be able to shoot or pass to (5) inside the zone. Also shown in Diagram 6-19 is (4)'s clear to the corner.

If (3) is not open, (2) has two options. He may: (A) pass to (4) in the corner, or (B) pass back to (1), who has moved back to the point for the reverse option.

(A) The Pass to (4)

When (2) passes to (4), (3) slides down the lane, looking for a pass and then clears across the lane to form a natural screen for (5), who cuts ballside and attempts to find a hole in the zone. See Diagram 6-20.

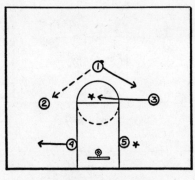

Diagram 6-19

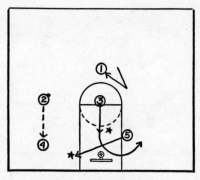

Diagram 6-20

If (4) passes to (5), he screens and attempts to trap the zone inside as (2) moves to the open area. See Diagram 6-21.

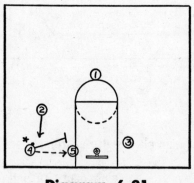

Diagram 6-21

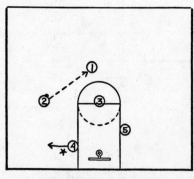

Diagram 6-22

(B) The Reverse Option

This play is keyed when (2) returns the ball to (1) once he has determined that (3) is not open on his cut to the middle. See Diagram 6-22.

Seeing this pass, (3) moves quickly down the lane and around the downscreen by (5). See Diagram 6-23.

As soon as (3) catches the ball, the sequence is repeated on that side of the court. See Diagram 6-24.

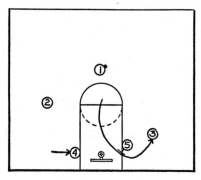
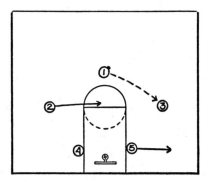

Diagram 6-23   **Diagram 6-24**

This second-time-around move very often leads to a pass in the middle to (2), followed by a pass to (4) for a power lay-up. See Diagram 6-25.

This man-to-man play is especially strong against zones because it tests them in their most vulnerable areas—the corner and the middle.

THE GUARD CHOICE PLAY

As point guard (1) brings the ball up court, (2) (the man who took the ball out for (1)) cuts down the lane. He ((2)) may cut around the double screen formed by (5) and (3), or around (4). See Diagram 6-26.

First Option Around the Double Stack

(2) cuts down the lane and around the double stack. This cut may trap the zone inside and result in an easy jump shot for (2). See Diagram 6-27.

If (2) is not open, (1) looks for (3), who cuts across the lane and around (4)'s downscreen. (1) can facilitate (3) being open if he fakes a pass to (2), to pull the zone in that direction, and then passes to (3). See Diagram 6-28.

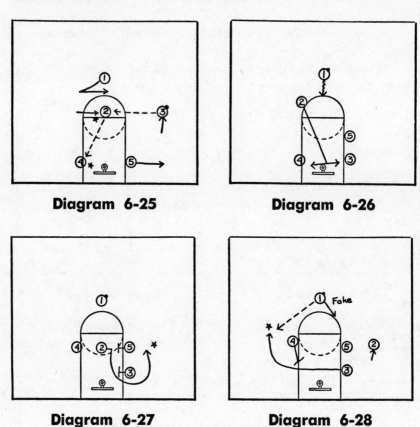

Diagram 6-25   Diagram 6-26

Diagram 6-27   Diagram 6-28

NOTE: This pressure on the zone perimeter will sometimes leave a hole in the middle of the zone and permit (1) to pass directly to (5) for a power lay-up shot. See Diagram 6-29.

Second Option Around the Single Screen

This time, (2) chooses to cut around (4) and receive a single screen. See Diagram 6-30.

If (2) is not open, (3) pops out of (5)'s downscreen. See Diagram 6-31.

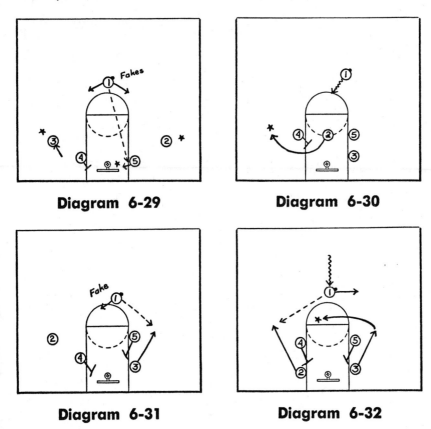

Diagram 6-29   **Diagram 6-30**

Diagram 6-31   **Diagram 6-32**

The following play is primarily a zone play that fits very well with a stacking man-to-man offense.

A STACKING ZONE CONTINUITY

This zone continuity offense is built around stack plays. The offense begins as (2) and (3) pop out of downscreens by (4) and (5). In Diagram 6-32, (1) passes to (2) and this tells (3) to cut to the middle free-throw line high. If (3) is open, (2) passes to him and he may shoot or pass to (4) or (5) inside the zone. Note that after (1) passed to (2), he moved to the other side of the lane.

If (3) is not open, (4) cuts to the corner and (2) passes to him. (2) then cuts to the ballside low post area. See Diagram 6-33.

If (2) was not open, (3) steps out and receives a pass from (4). See Diagram 6-34.

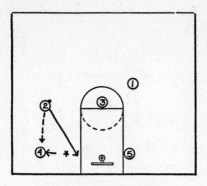

Diagram 6-33

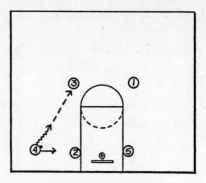

Diagram 6-34

(3) then passes to (1). This pass tells (2) to cut across the lane and loop around (5)'s downscreen. (4) moves toward the lane. See Diagram 6-35.

After passing to (1), (3) loops down and around (4), who is moving toward the lane. If (1) cannot pass to (2), he dribbles to the other side and looks for (3). See Diagram 6-36.

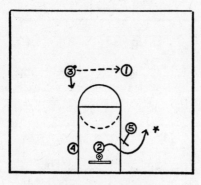

Diagram 6-35

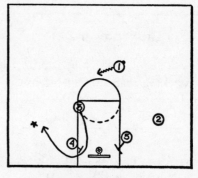

Diagram 6-36

(1) may pass to either new wing man, and the opposite wing will cut to the middle to restart the continuity. In Diagram 6-37, (1) passes to (3).

Some special options that may be run within the context of this continuity follow.

Diagram 6-37

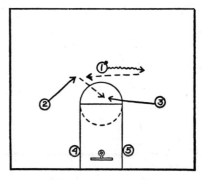

Diagram 6-38

THE QUICK TRIANGLE OPTION

Point man (1) dribbles away from (2). This pulls (2) out front to receive a pass from (1). This tells (3) to cut to the middle. See Diagram 6-38.

(3) may shoot, or pass inside to (4) or (5). As (3) received the pass from (2), (1) cut down and became the third option. See Diagram 6-39.

Once (1) receives the ball at the wing, (5) cuts to the corner and the basic continuity is run. See Diagrams 6-40 through 6-42.

THE QUICK REVERSAL OPTION

At the point where a big man ((4) in Diagram 6-43) cuts to the corner and receives a pass from a wing man, the quick reversal option

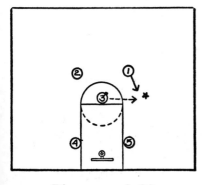

Diagram 6-39

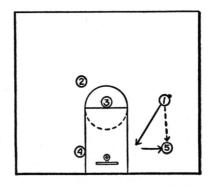

Diagram 6-40

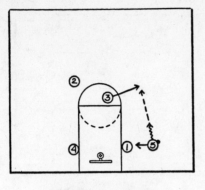

Diagram 6-41

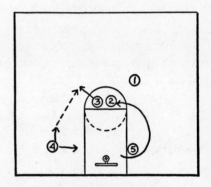

Diagram 6-42

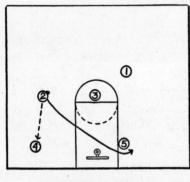
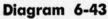

Diagram 6-43

Diagram 6-44

may be run. When (2) cuts down, he does not stop in the ballside low post area. Instead, he goes directly across the lane and loops around (5) to the free-throw line area.

(3) steps out, takes a pass from (4), and looks for (2) in the middle. See Diagram 6-44.

If (3) can pass to (2), (2) can shoot or look for (4) or (5) inside the zone. See Diagram 6-45.

If (3) cannot pass to (2), he passes to (1), and the continuity goes on.

THE ZONE BACKDOOR PASS OPTION

Anytime point man (1) has the ball, the far inside man ((4) in Diagram 6-46), may break to the free-throw line area and receive a pass.

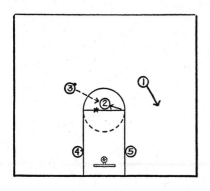
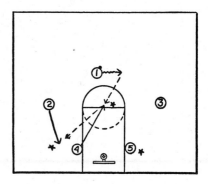

Diagram 6-45   **Diagram 6-46**

This tells the wing man on that side ((2)) to break down and receive a
pass from (4) for a possible jump shot.

Note that (5) may be open inside the zone.

· · · · · · · · ·

Stack
Motion Plays

· · · · · · · · · · · · · · · · · · · ·

SEVEN

• • • • • • • •

The Lob
and Loop Continuity

This continuity features downscreens, lob passes, and a looping action, and together they present the defense a variety of problems.

PERSONNEL ALIGNMENT

Players (1), (2), and (3) can be more or less the same type of player. They are mobile, strong jumpshooters and have the ability to read the defense. Player (1) should be the best at initiating the offense and resisting defensive pressure. Players (4) and (5) are big, can rebound, and are able to score in the post area. They also should be adequate ball handlers. See Diagram 7-1.

THE BASIC MOTION

After (1) has brought the ball into the front court and (2) and (3) have popped out of their respective downscreens, (1) may pass to either wing (as to (2) in Diagram 7-2). (1) then slashes off post man (5), who moved to the free-throw line area.

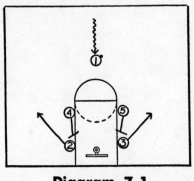
Diagram 7-1

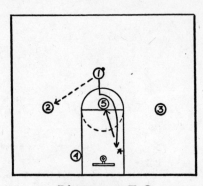
Diagram 7-2

If (1) is not open for a lob pass, (2) may pass to (4) in the ballside low post area, or pass to (5). If the pass is to (5), (1) loops around (3)'s downscreen and out to the wing position. (5) may then pass to (3) or (4) inside, or to (1) at the wing. See Diagrams 7-3 and 7-4.

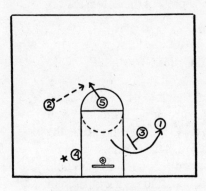
Diagram 7-3

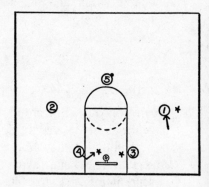
Diagram 7-4

In Diagram 7-5, (5) chooses to pass to (1) at the wing. When this occurs, (3) clears across the lane, (5) slides down to the ballside low post area, and (2) moves to the point.

(1) may then: (A) pass to (5) and split the post with (2) (see Diagram 7-6), or (B) pass to (2) who then reverses the ball to (3) coming out of (4)'s downscreen (see Diagram 7-7).

This pass from (2) to (3) starts the play again. In Diagram 7-8, (2) slashes off (5), who has cut to the free-throw line area.

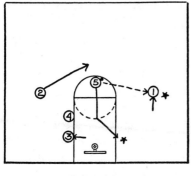

Diagram 7-5

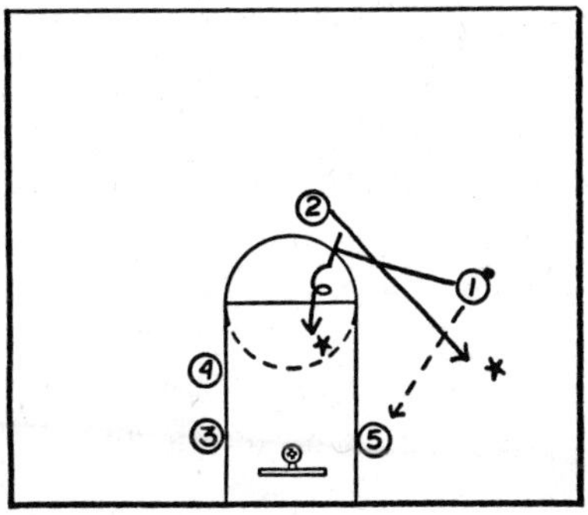

Diagram 7-6

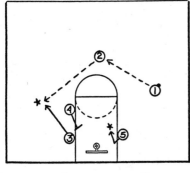

Diagram 7-7

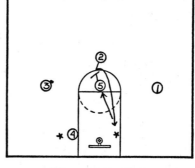

Diagram 7-8

While the lob and loop continuity is being run, several special options *may* be interjected. They include:

(A) The overload option.

(B) The pivot triangle option.

(C) The screen-away option.

(A) The Overload Option

After point man ((1) in Diagram 7-9) has passed to a wing man (2), he cuts toward (5) moving to the free-throw line area. This time, however, once it is obvious the lob is not open, he ((1)) loops to the ballside corner. He uses (4)'s downscreen to get open.

If (1) is not open, (2) may pass to (4) in the ballside low post area, or to (3), who has moved to the point after seeing (1)'s cut to the ballside. When the pass is made to (3), (5) slides back to his original position, (2) cuts through and around (5), and (1) replaces (2) at the wing. See Diagram 7-10.

This again balances the offensive set and a new play sequence may be run. See Diagram 7-11.

(B) The Pivot Triangle Option

As the lob and loop continuity is being run, the "pivot triangle option" may be interjected. This occurs when the point man ((1) in Diagram 7-12) passes to wing man (2) who has popped out of (4)'s downscreen. The offside post man (5) declares this option by not being at the free throw line as (1) cuts through. This tells (1) to come down and set a definite screen for him. (5) uses (1)'s screen and breaks to the head of the key.

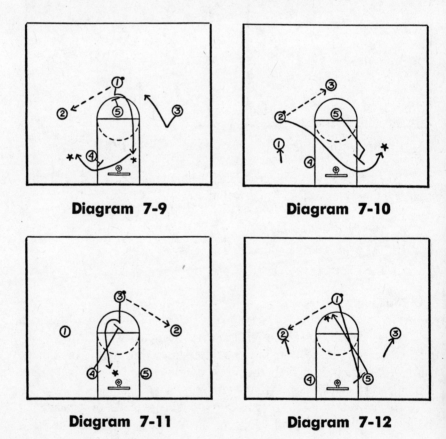

Diagram 7-9   Diagram 7-10

Diagram 7-11   Diagram 7-12

(2) looks inside for (4) in the ballside low post area, and if he is not open, passes to (5). If X4 had been fronting (4), (5) may be able to get the ball to him for a power lay-up. See Diagram 7-13.

If (4) is not open, (5) reverses the ball to (3) at the wing position. This tells (1) to screen away for (4), who cuts to the ballside low post area. See Diagram 7-14.

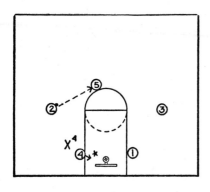

Diagram 7-13   **Diagram 7-14**

(5) then moves down and screens for (1), who cuts to the head of the key. This quick screening of the screener ((1)) will very often provide (1) an easy shot or leave (4) open inside. If not, (1) may pass to either wing and the lob and loop continuity is resumed. See Diagrams 7-15 through 7-19.

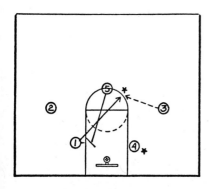

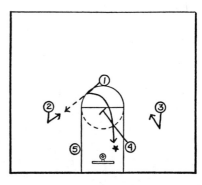

Diagram 7-15   **Diagram 7-16**

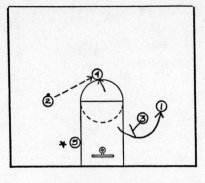

Diagram 7-17   Diagram 7-18

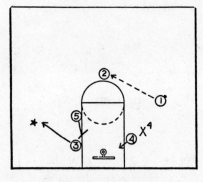
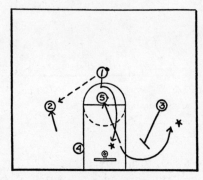

Diagram 7-19   Diagram 7-20

(C) The Screen-Away Option

The basic lob and loop action may be run with a screen-away option. In Diagram 7-20, after (1) passes to (2) and cuts off (5)'s screen, he again loops around (3)'s downscreen.

This time, however, after (5) passes to (1), he screens away for (2), who cuts to the point. At the same time, (3) screens away for (4), who moves to the ballside post area. See Diagram 7-21.

(1) may: (A) pass to (4) and split the post with (2) (see Diagram 7-22), or (B) pass to (2) at the point. (2) then shoots or restarts the lob and loop continuity. See Diagrams 7-23 and 7-24.

Note that (4) and (5) continue to be the post men as the offense is run again.

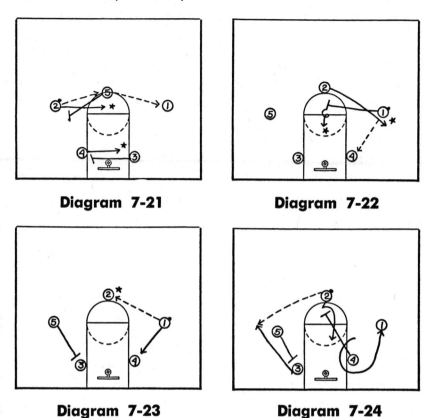

Diagram 7-21   Diagram 7-22

Diagram 7-23   Diagram 7-24

THE LOB AND LOOP CONTINUITY WITH A TRIANGLE OPTION

Another way to use the lob and loop continuity with a triangle option is as follows:

In Diagram 7-25, (1) passes to (2) and cuts over the high post screen of (5).

If (1) is not open, he loops around (3)'s downscreen. (5) then steps out, takes a pass from (2), and passes to (1). See Diagram 7-26.

At this point, the triangle option is run. (3) screens away for (4), who cuts to the ball. See Diagram 7-27.

(5) then screens down for (3), who cuts to the head of the key. (1) looks first for (4) and, if he is not open, passes to (3). From that point, (3) may pass to either wing and a new play is run. See Diagrams 7-28 and 7-29.

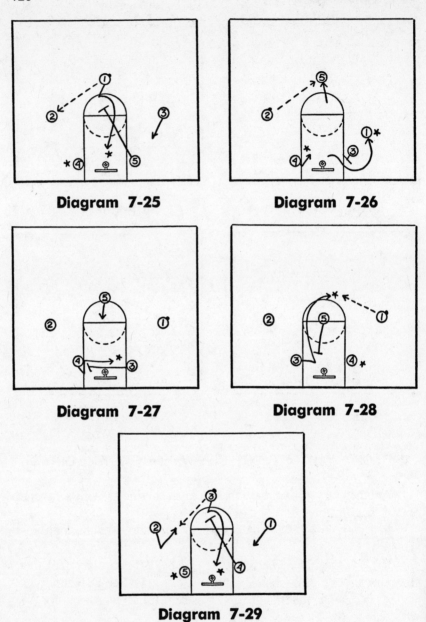

Diagram 7-25   Diagram 7-26

Diagram 7-27   Diagram 7-28

Diagram 7-29

THE FIVE-MAN INTERCHANGEABLE LOB
AND LOOP CONTINUITY

If a coach lacks post men and desires a five-man motion, he may
run this five-man interchangeable continuity.

In Diagram 7-30, (1) passes to (2) and again cuts off (5)'s screen for a possible lob pass. If (1) is not open, (5) steps out, receives a pass from (2), and reverses it to (1) cutting around (3)'s downscreen. See Diagram 7-31.

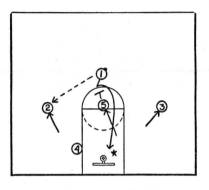
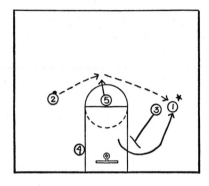

Diagram 7-30   **Diagram 7-31**

At this point, the five-man interchangeable continuity differs from the basic pattern. (5), after passing to (1), cuts off a screen by (4) (who has moved to the free-throw line area) for a possible lob pass. See Diagram 7-32.

If (5) is not open for the lob pass, (4) steps out to the head of the key, receives a pass from (1), and reverses to (5), looping around (2)'s downscreen. See Diagram 7-33.

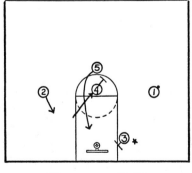

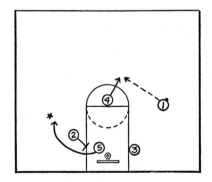

Diagram 7-32   **Diagram 7-33**

If (5) was not open for a shot, the continuity would go on. See Diagrams 7-34 through 7-36.

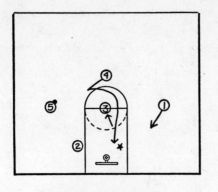

Diagram 7-34   **Diagram 7-35**

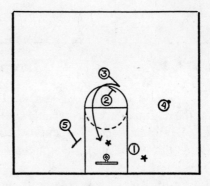

Diagram 7-36

This five-man interchangeable continuity would go on until:

- The lob pass is open.
- Someone gets open looping around a downscreen, or
- Someone is open in the ballside low post area.

The special options, including the pivot triangle, screen-away, and overload, may also be used in conjunction with this five-man motion.

EIGHT

· · · · · · · · ·

Auxiliary Stack
Motion Plays

The stack maneuver was originally designed to take advantage of the talents of a strong jump shooter and a powerful inside man. Since that time, smaller teams have found they may use the stack play without giving away too much inside by utilizing it to initiate their motion, or by integrating it into their motion plays. Following are four movement-oriented offenses that include the stack maneuver. They are:

A. The "Three-Man Motion Offense" which is designed for three mobile players and two pivot men who must stay close to the basket to be effective.

B. "The Crossing Post Offense" which is also most functional for a team with three mobile players and two limited big men.

C. "A Simple Stack Motion" which is an easily taught five-man interchangeable continuity.

D. "A U.C.L.A. Type Continuity" designed around stacks, slash cuts, and downscreens.

Additional options are offered with each of the offenses that may be used to give the pattern depth or to meet specific situations.

THE THREE-MAN MOTION OFFENSE

If the coach desires a three-man motion with two fairly stationary post men, the following offense may suffice.

Personnel Alignment

The point man (1) initiates the play by passing to one of the wing men ((2) or (3)) as they come out of downscreens set by the two post men ((4) and (5)). See Diagram 8-1.

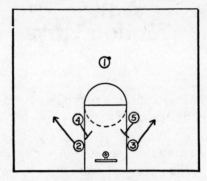

Diagram 8-1

After wing men (2) and (3) come out of the stacks, a pass and move away game is utilized that includes:

(A) A pass and screen-away.

(B) A pass and loop around the offside post man.

(C) A dribble chase rule.

(D) A pass to the post and split rule.

When using these rules, the following play situations may evolve:

(1) passes to (2) and screens away for (3), who moves to the point. As (2) receives the ball, he attempts to get the ball in to (4). If he can do so, he splits the post with (3). See Diagrams 8-2 and 8-3.

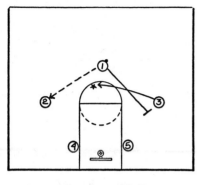

Diagram 8-2

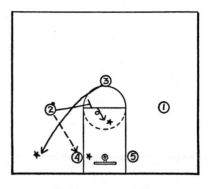

Diagram 8-3

If X4 denies (2)'s pass to (4) by fronting him, the pass is made to (3). (3) may shoot or look inside to (4), who attempts to pin his defender (X4) outside and be open for a power lay-up shot. See Diagram 8-4.

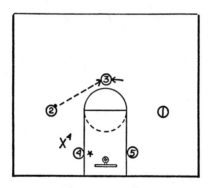

Diagram 8-4

If the defense is very strong and (2) can pass to neither (4) nor (3), he resorts to the dribble chase. He does this by dribbling toward (3) and clearing him down and around the post man on the open side ((4)). (4) can facilitate this move by downscreening as (3) loops around him. This move, in effect, is a stack maneuver. (2) may then pass to either wing and continue the motion. See Diagrams 8-5 and 8-6.

Note in the previous diagram that (1) made a change of direction to get open.

In Diagram 8-7, (2) chooses to pass to (1) and move toward (3)'s side. He does this by cutting down and around (4)'s downscreen.

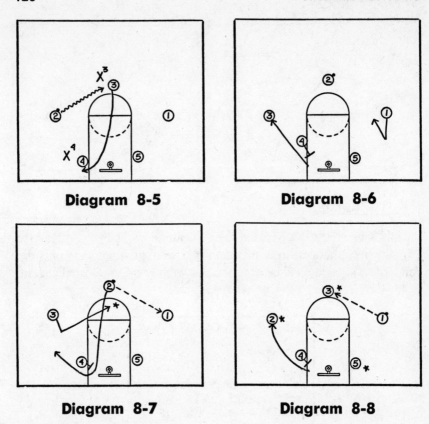

Diagram 8-5   **Diagram 8-6**

Diagram 8-7   **Diagram 8-8**

(1) may, at this point, pass to (5) and split the post with (3), pass to (3) at the point, or dribble at (3) and chase him to the open corner. In Diagram 8-8, the pass is made to (3).

If, during this pass and move away motion by players (1), (2), and (3), a pass is made from the point to a post man, the split rule is in effect, but a backdoor option is added. When (3) passes to post man (4), it tells wing man (2) to backdoor his defender and look for a pass from (4). See Diagram 8-9.

If (2) is not open, he stops and waits for (3) to come down and screen for him. (2) uses (3)'s screen to move back for a possible jump shot. After screening, (3) clears across the lane. See Diagram 8-10.

If neither (2) nor (3) is open, (1) moves toward the ball, receives a pass from (4), and reverses it to (3), moving out of (5)'s downscreen. See Diagram 8-11.

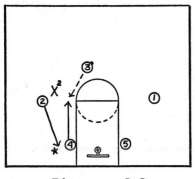

Diagram 8-9

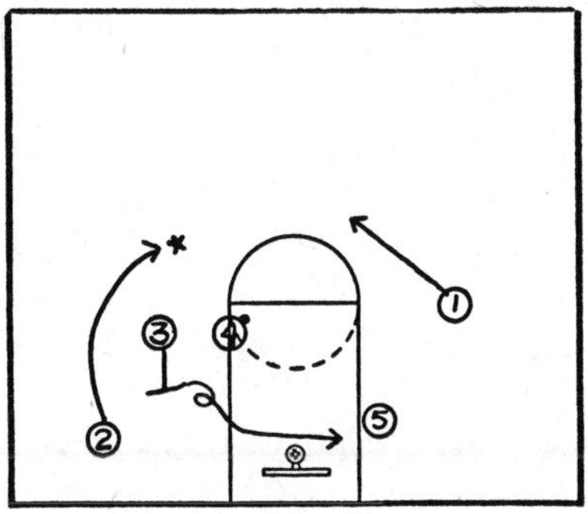

Diagram 8-10

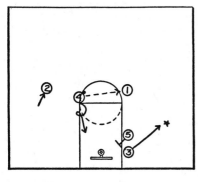

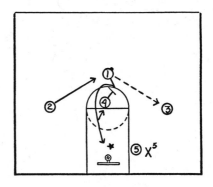

Diagram 8-11

Diagram 8-12

During this simple but productive motion, the following special options may be run:

(A) The lob option.

(B) The switch play.

(C) The dribble reverse action.

(D) The overload option.

(E) The post screen away option.

(A) The Lob Pass Option

The lob pass is keyed by the post man away from the man receiving the pass from (1) (see post man (4) in Diagram 8-12). As (1) passes to (3), post man (4) moves up to the free-throw line area and blindscreens (1)'s defender (X1).

(1) sees (4)'s screen and cuts over him to the basket, looking for a pass from (3).

If the lob pass is not open, (3) may: (A) pass to (5) and split the post with (2); (B) pass to (2) moving to the point (this pass balances the offense and allows for a new play to be run); (C) use the option of dribbling at (2) and chasing him to the open corner. If the lob pass is not made, (4) moves back to his original position.

(B) The Switch Option

If the ballside post man is alert and notices that the defense is switching on lateral screens, he may key the "switch option." In Diagram 8-13, post man (5) notices that the defenders on (1), (2), and (3) are switching. He takes advantage of this by cutting to the offside high post area and calling out "switch."

This tells (2) to cut low off (4) and move to the ballside lay-up area. He then receives a pass from (3) for an easy lay-up shot. See Diagram 8-14.

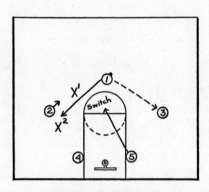

Diagram 8-13

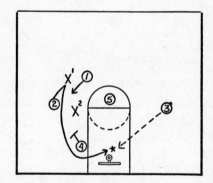

Diagram 8-14

(C) The Dribble Reverse Option

This play is called by the point man ((1) in Diagram 8-15), who dribbles at wing man (2) and clears him down and across the lane. (1) then looks to post man (4).

If (1) passes to (4), he splits the post with (3). See Diagram 8-16.

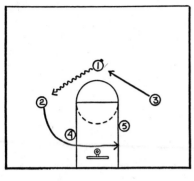   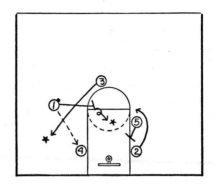

Diagram 8-15   **Diagram 8-16**

If (1) passes to (3), he reverses the ball to (2), popping out of a stack formed by (5)'s downscreen. See Diagram 8-17.

(D) The Overload Option

At times during the basic three-man motion, a cutter will move to the ballside corner. See (1) in Diagram 8-18.

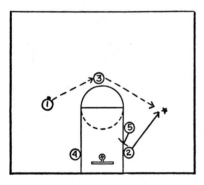   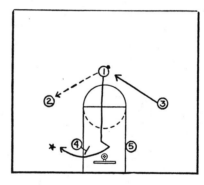

Diagram 8-17   **Diagram 8-18**

When this occurs, (2) may:

(A) Pass to (4) and screen for (1). (3) would then backdoor his defender. See Diagram 8-19.

(B) Pass to (4) and screen for (3). (1) would then backdoor his defender. See Diagram 8-20.

(C) Dribble at (3) to balance the offense and continue the motion. See Diagrams 8-21 and 8-22.

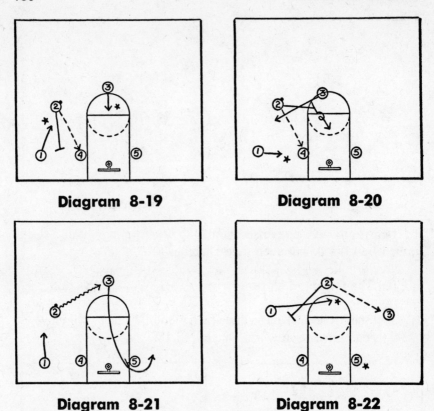

Diagram 8-19   **Diagram 8-20**

Diagram 8-21   **Diagram 8-22**

(E) The Post Screen-Away Option

If some additional motion is desired of the post men ((4) and (5)), the "Post Screen-Away" option may be run. In Diagram 8-23, the post man on the ballside screens away for the offside post man (5). (5) cuts to the ballside low post area. After his screen-away, (4) pops back to the ballside high post area.

If (2) passes to (5) in the low post, (5) may shoot or look for (2) and (3) splitting off him. See Diagram 8-24.

If (2) passes to (4) in the high post, (4) may shoot, look for (1) and (2)'s splitting action, or look for (5) inside. If they are not open, he ((4)) may reverse the ball directly to (1) on the offside wing. When this happens, (5) makes a reverse pivot and cuts low to (1)'s side. (5) might be open because when (4) had the ball and looked inside, (5)'s de-

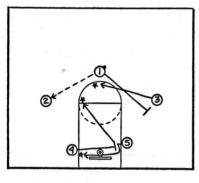 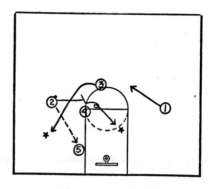

Diagram 8-23   **Diagram 8-24**

fender (X5) probably played him ballside and high to deny the pass. See Diagram 8-25.

Note that (2) and (3) split the post after (2)'s pass to (4). This presents scoring opportunities and also keeps the defense busy.

The preceding offense is designed for a team with two big men ((4) and (5)) with average skills and three small movers ((1), (2), and (3)). If a team desires more motion from its post men, the following offense may be used.

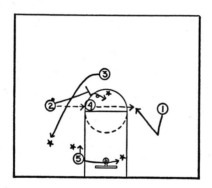

Diagram 8-25

THE CROSSING POST MEN OFFENSE

The moves of (1), (2), and (3) are very much the same as the ones they used in the previous offense. However, post men (4) and (5) play high and low post positions on the same side of the lane and utilize a crossing action as they move to the ball. The combination of the pass and move away action of (1), (2), and (3), when combined with the crossing action of post men (4) and (5), result in many interesting play situations. Some examples are the:

(A) High to low post passes.

(B) Lobs to the point man.

(C) Crossing post motion.

(D) Post side dribble.

(E) Open side dribble chase.

(F) Popping stack.

(A) High- to Low-Post Pass Option

In Diagram 8-26, (1) passes to (2) and moves to (3)'s side by way of a looping action around post men (4) and (5). (4) and (5) cross as they move to the ballside.

If X4 fronts (4) in the low post area, (2) passes to (5) who looks inside to (4). See Diagram 8-27.

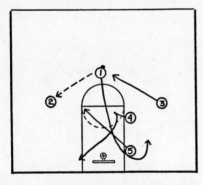

Diagram 8-26

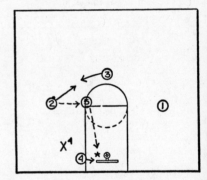

Diagram 8-27

(2) then splits the high post with (3). It should be noted that (2) is very often open in his cut over (5). See Diagram 8-28.

(B) Lob to the Point Man Option

This option is built into the combination of rules. In Diagram 8-29, after (1) passes to (2), post men (4) and (5) move to the ballside

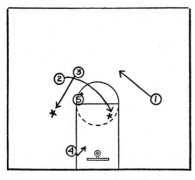

Diagram 8-28

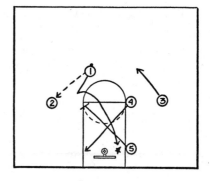

Diagram 8-29

in their crossing maneuver. (1) may use this motion by stepping toward (2) and cutting off (5) as he moves to the ballside high post area. (2) may then lob to (1).

If (1) is not open, (2) uses his other options.

(C) The Crossing Post Motion

As (4) and (5) move to the ballside, the second cutter has the best chance of getting open. He does this by making a change of direction and cutting close to his partner (5). Diagram 8-30 shows (4) as the second cutter getting open off (5)'s cut.

Diagram 8-31 shows (5) getting open off (4)'s cut.

The post men must learn to work together and sense each other's moves. This is done through hard work and functional drilling in practice.

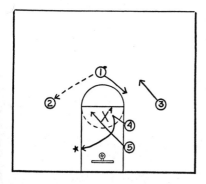

Diagram 8-30

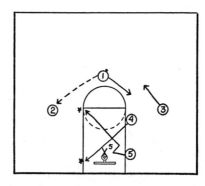

Diagram 8-31

(D) The Post Side Dribble Chase Option

When point man (1) dribble-chases the wing man on the double post side (see wing man (2) in Diagram 8-32), it keys him to loop around the double post and to the point.

(1) then passes to (2) and cuts over (4) and (5) for a possible return pass. See Diagram 8-33.

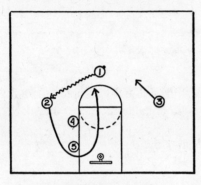

Diagram 8-32   **Diagram 8-33**

If (1) is not open, (4) screens down for (5) and (1) continues across the lane to receive a downscreen from (3). See Diagram 8-34.

(E) Open Side Dribble Chase Option

When point man (1) chooses to make a dribble-chase to the side away from the post men (open side), the following play action results. (3), the wing man on the open side, clears across the lane and around post men (4) and (5) as they move to the ballside. (See Diagram 8-35.)

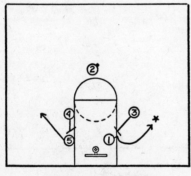
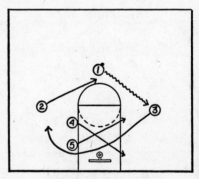

Diagram 8-34   **Diagram 8-35**

It is very easy for X3 to get lost in the traffic caused by all this movement. (1) may then: reverse the ball to (3) by way of (2) (see Diagram 8-36); pass the ball to (4) or (5), and split the post with (2) (see Diagrams 8-37 and 8-38); or save his dribble and dribble at (2) to clear him to balance the offense. See Diagram 8-39.

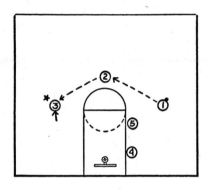

Diagram 8-36

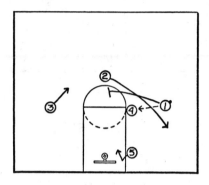

Diagram 8-37

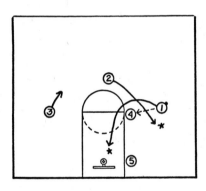

Diagram 8-38

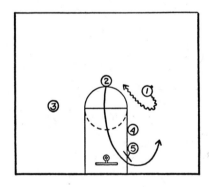

Diagram 8-39

(F) Popping the Stack Option

When the ball is entered to the wing on the double post stack side ((2) in Diagram 8-40), the post men may pop the stack. All this amounts to is the top man ((4)) in the stack downscreening for the bottom man ((5)) who "pops" inside to the ballside free-throw line area.

(5) may be open off (4)'s downscreen. If a switch occurs, (4) may be open in the low post area for a pass from either (2) or (5). See Diagrams 8-41 and 8-42.

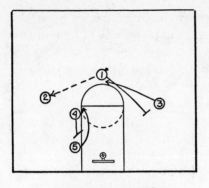

Diagram 8-40   **Diagram 8-41**

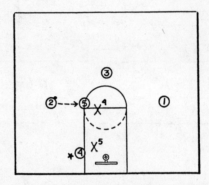

Diagram 8-42

IMPORTANT NOTE: Not all of these specials can or should be run at one given point in the season. They should be used when and if variety is needed, or to take advantage of specific situations.

A SIMPLE STACK MOTION OFFENSE

Perhaps the most often used, but nevertheless, functional stack motion offense consists of two rules:

(A) When a pass is made from the point to a wing (as from (1) to (2) in Diagram 8-43), both onside offensive players (1) and (4) screen away.

(B) When a wing man ((2)) passes to the point ((3)), both wing men ((2) and (1)) screen down for the post man on their respective side. See Diagram 8-44.

These rules result in a five-man interchangeable continuity.

If the coach desires to keep his big men ((4) and (5)) inside, the following adjustment may be made.

The pass to a wing from the point ((1) to (3) in Diagram 8-45) still keys the two screens away.

However, when a pass is made from a wing man to the point (as (3) to (2) in Diagram 8-46), the two wing men, instead of downscreening for the post men on their side, loop around them and back out to the wing.

For variety, they may cross the lane and pop out of a downscreen set by the post man on that side. See Diagram 8-47.

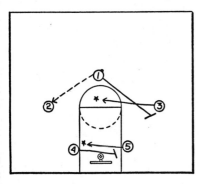

Diagram 8-43

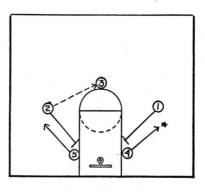

Diagram 8-44

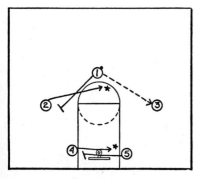

Diagram 8-45

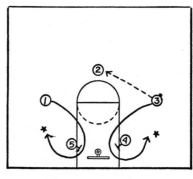

Diagram 8-46

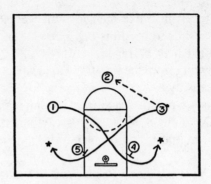

Diagram 8-47

A UCLA TYPE CONTINUITY STACK MOTION

The play begins as point man (1) dribbles to the side of the court on which the stack of (4) and (2) is located. (2) then pops out of (4)'s downscreen and receives a pass. The offside stack ((5) and (3)) does not move. See Diagram 8-48.

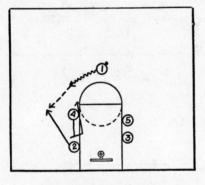

Diagram 8-48

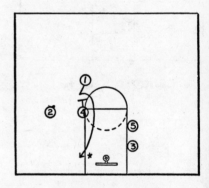

Diagram 8-49

(1) then makes a UCLA-type slash cut off (4) to the ballside low post area, looking for a return pass from (2). See Diagram 8-49.

(4) then steps out and gets a pass from (2). (2) screens down for (1), who pops out looking for a pass from (4). See Diagram 8-50.

If (4) cannot get the ball to (1) or (2), (3) pops out front, off (5)'s downscreen. (4) passes to (3) and (1) cuts high off (2), looking for a pass from (3). See Diagram 8-51.

Diagram 8-50

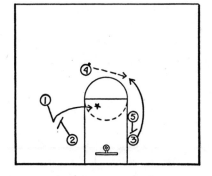

Diagram 8-51

In the event (1) is not open, he loops down and around (5)'s downscreen and receives a pass from (3). See Diagram 8-52.

(1) can shoot or look for (3) making the slash cut to the ballside low post area. Note that (5) moved up to set the screen for (3). See Diagram 8-53.

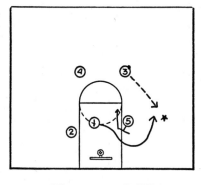

Diagram 8-52

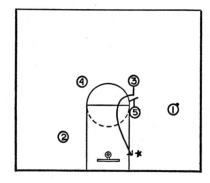

Diagram 8-53

From there, the continuity may be repeated. See Diagrams 8-54 through 8-56.

This continuity allows a small team to run a UCLA type play while moving the defense.

These four offenses permit a coach to choose the ideas that best fit his personnel. This would vary from featuring a strong inside stacking, posting-up game to quick-hitting stacks run from moving continuities.

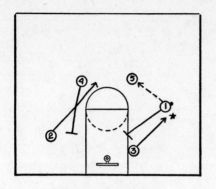

Diagram 8-54

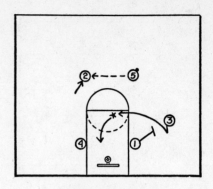

Diagram 8-55

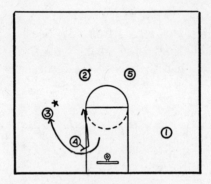

Diagram 8-56

NINE

. . . .

Stack Motion Offenses
Versus Zone Defenses

The stack motion type man-to-man offense may be used successfully against zone defenses. Many of the man-to-man plays mentioned earlier in Chapters Seven and Eight are adaptable for use against zone defenses.

THE THREE-MAN MOTION OFFENSE

Loop the Post Option

The three-man pass and move away game mentioned in Chapter Seven is an excellent zone offense. In Diagram 9-1, (1) passes to (2) and goes opposite, down, and around the offside post man (5). (5) attempts to pin the zone inside and keep it from covering (1), as the ball is reversed back to (1) by way of (3), who cut to the point. See Diagram 9-1.

This screening of the overshift presents many problems for the zone.

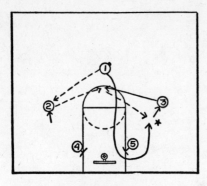

Diagram 9-1

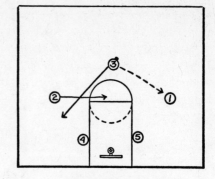

Diagram 9-2

Flash the Middle Option

Using the same basic idea, (3) passes to (1) and screens away for (2). (2) flashes to the middle and looks for a pass from (1). See Diagram 9-2.

If (2) gets a pass from (1), he shoots or looks for (4) or (5) inside the zone. See Diagram 9-3.

If (2) is not open, he loops back around post man (4) and the ball is reversed to him by way of (3), who doubled back to the point. See Diagram 9-4.

Note that (4) screened the zone and disallowed it to shift back to cover (2).

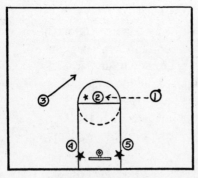

Diagram 9-3

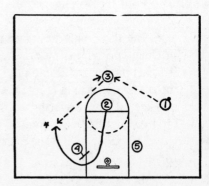

Diagram 9-4

Cross-Court Lob Option

Another pass and screen-away maneuver is the offside screen. In Diagram 9-5, (1) passes to (3). As this pass is made, (2) moves up and screens the front zone player nearest to him. (1) then cuts away from his pass and utilizes (2)'s screen to receive a cross-court pass from (3) for a jump shot.

Overload Option

If (1) desires to create an overload, he may pass to (3) and cut down and around (5) to the ballside corner. See Diagram 9-6.

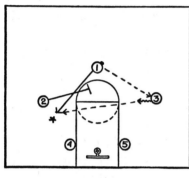

Diagram 9-5

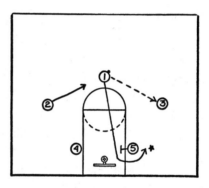

Diagram 9-6

(1), (3), (2), and (5) then utilize the triangles formed by the overload until (3) decides to balance the offense. He does this with a dribble chase. He dribbles at (2), who clears down and around (4). See Diagram 9-7.

Note that (1) moved up to replace (3).

Wing Dribble Chase

A second type of dribble chase is used when the point man ((1) in Diagram 9-8) dribbles at wing man (2). This clears (2) down and around both post men ((4) and (5)). (3) then moves to the point, receives a pass from (1), and passes the ball to (2), who utilized (5)'s downscreen to get open.

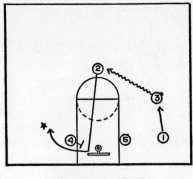

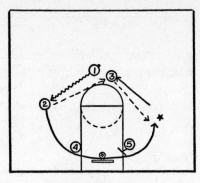

Diagram 9-7   **Diagram 9-8**

If an overload had been desired, (2) could have stopped in the ballside corner. See Diagram 9-9.

Again, the triangles formed by the overload would be utilized until the offense is balanced by another dribble chase. See (1) in Diagrams 9-10 and 9-11.

THE CROSSING POST OFFENSE

The crossing post offense utilizes the same three-man motion plays, but adds the post movement. This crossing of the posts leads to the following additional zone offense opportunities.

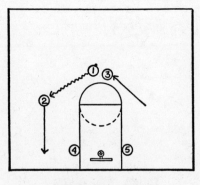

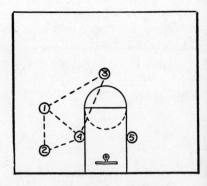

Diagram 9-9   **Diagram 9-10**

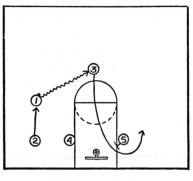

Diagram 9-11

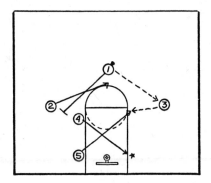

Diagram 9-12

High-Post to Low-Post Pass

In Diagram 9-12, (1) passes to (3) and screens away for (2), who moves to the ball. At the same time, post men (4) and (5) move to the ball side in a crossing maneuver. (3) may pass to either (4), (5), or (2).

(A) The Pass to the High Post (5)

If he chooses to pass to (5) cutting to the high post area, (5) quickly looks inside for (4) in the low post area.

If (4) is not open, (5) can reverse the ball to (1) in the offside wing area. See Diagram 9-13.

When this happens, the posts again move to the ball side in their crossing action. See Diagram 9-14.

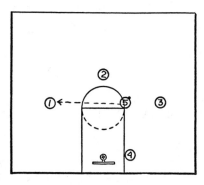

Diagram 9-13

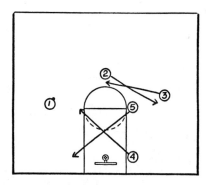

Diagram 9-14

(B) The Pass to the Low Post (4)

When (3) passes to (4) in the low post area, high post man (5) cuts down, hoping to find a hole in the zone and receive a pass from (4). See Diagram 9-15.

(C) The Pass to the Point (2)

If (3) passes back to (2), the pass and move-away action of (1), (2), and (3) continues as does the crossing maneuver by post men (4) and (5). See Diagram 9-16.

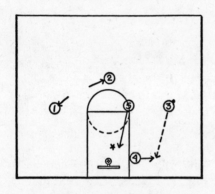
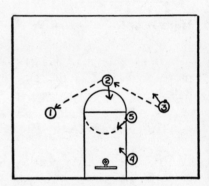

Diagram 9-15   **Diagram 9-16**

The crossing action of (4) and (5) also enhances the chance of a point man getting open when he passes away from and loops around the post men. In Diagram 9-17, (1) passes to (2) and moves toward (3)'s side by looping around (4) and (5), who are crossing as they move toward the ballside.

The zone players are often too concerned with the cuts of (4) and (5) and can be caught by a quick reversal to (1) by way of (3). See Diagram 9-18.

Also, it is possible that their zone slides may be impeded by the offensive movement.

The Corner Play

Another fine option that may be used at the point where (3) had the ball back in Diagram 9-16 is the corner play. (4), the low post man,

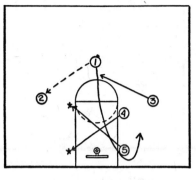

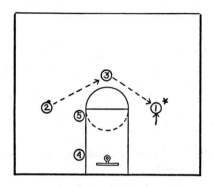

Diagram 9-17   **Diagram 9-18**

could have cut to the corner and received a pass from (3). (5) would then slide down to the low post area, hoping a hole in the zone was created when it elongated to cover the corner. See Diagram 9-19.

(3), (4), and (5) may then utilize the triangle to work the zone. However, once the ball is passed to (2), the motion is resumed. See Diagram 9-20.

Note that (4) moved to the high post after (3) passed to (2).

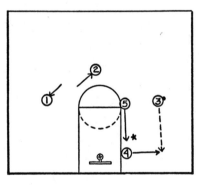
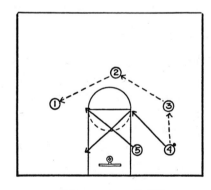

Diagram 9-19   **Diagram 9-20**

THE LOB AND LOOP CONTINUITY

As (2) pops out of (4)'s downscreen and receives a pass from (1), (5) cuts to the high post area. (1) cuts down the lane and may cut to either side. See Diagram 9-21.

(A) If he cuts to the far side around (3), it amounts to a screen of the overshift. See Diagram 9-22.

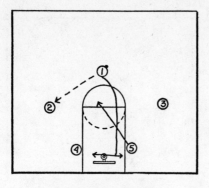

Diagram 9-21   **Diagram 9-22**

(B) If (1) cuts down the lane and to the ballside, it is an overload. See Diagram 9-23.

(A) The Overshifted Screen Option

(1) cuts down the lane (as in Diagram 9-24) and the offside wing man (3) attempts to pin the zone in the lane by screening down for him. The ball is then reversed from (2) to (5) to (1) coming off (3)'s downscreen.

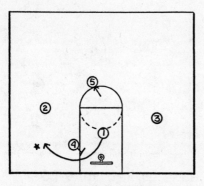
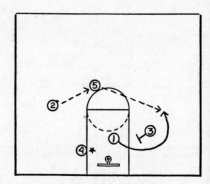

Diagram 9-23   **Diagram 9-24**

In the diagram above, (5) should look inside to (4) before reversing the ball to (1).

If (1) receives the ball and is not open, (3) clears the ballside post area to stack under (4), and (5) slides down looking for a pass. See Diagram 9-25.

If (5) is not open, (1) passes to (2) out front, who reverses the ball to (3), moving out of (4)'s downscreen. See Diagram 9-26.

This pass from the point ((2)) to a wing ((3)) keys a second round of the continuity. See Diagram 9-27.

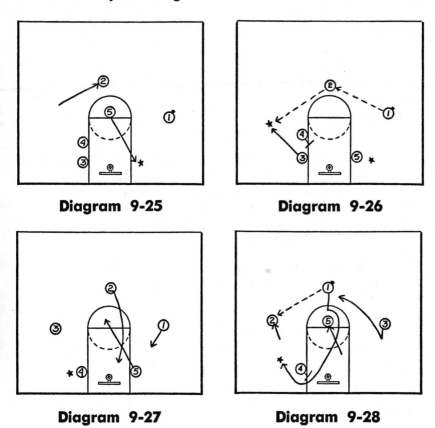

Diagram 9-25   Diagram 9-26

Diagram 9-27   Diagram 9-28

(B) The Overload Screen Option

This time, (1) (the point man in Diagram 9-28) passes to a wing, (2), cuts down the lane, and chooses to loop around onside post man (4). This keys the overload screen.

The players then utilize the overload triangles by passing and looking for shots until (2) wants to balance the offense. He may do this by passing to the point, (3), and clearing to the offside wing (see Diagram 9-29), or by dribbling at (3) and clearing him down the lane to the offside wing area (see Diagram 9-30).

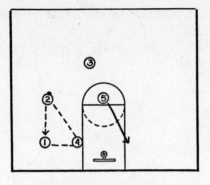

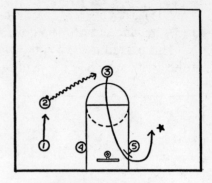

Diagram 9-29   **Diagram 9-30**

From there, either option (overshift or overload) may be run.

These motion offenses give the smaller team, desiring more movement, a functional man-to-man plan that may be adapted to face zone defenses. This makes these offenses valuable against defenses: that change on keys, that are combinations of zone and man-to-man, and/or are disguised so that it is hard to read whether they are zone or man-to-man.

· · · · · · · · · ·

SECTION FOUR

Special Game Situations
and Final Comments

· · · · · · · · · · · · · · · · · · · ·

TEN

• • • • • • • •

Special
Game Situations

This chapter deals with the special game situation techniques that often provide the margin of victory. They include: (1) out-of-bounds from the side, (2) out-of-bounds under your basket, (3) stalling plays, (4) the free throw situation, both offensively and defensively, (5) last second shot versus zone or man-to-man, (6) full court and sideline short time plays, and (7) the jump ball situation.

OUT-OF-BOUNDS PLAYS

Sideline Out-of-Bounds Play

Guard Choice

The ideal is to use an out-of-bounds that relates well to your basic offense. This cuts down on the time required to teach it and usually leads to better execution.

153

For this out-of-bounds play, the ball is taken out by weakside guard (1). The other four players line up on the free throw lane with (2) stacked inside, (5) on the ballside, (3) stacked inside, and (4) on the far side. See Diagram 10-1.

As the ball is handed to (1) by the referee, (5) screens down for (2) who pops out to the ballside head of the key. The path taken by (2) will be determined by how tight X2 plays him when he lines up. If X2 is tight on (2) and can be screened by (5), (2) swings through the lane and to the ball. See Diagram 10-2.

If X2 plays loose and anticipates (2)'s cut, (2) will have to use good judgment and may cut directly to the ball. See Diagram 10-3.

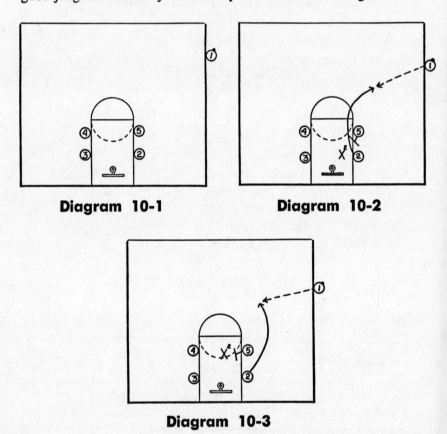

Diagram 10-1　　　　　**Diagram 10-2**

Diagram 10-3

If X2 beats (2) to the ball, (5) must step out, take a pass, and give it to (2). See Diagrams 10-4 and 10-5.

After (2) has the ball, (1) cuts through and has two options:

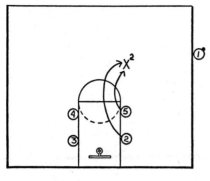
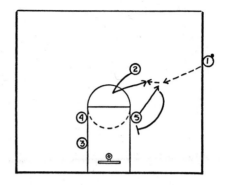

Diagram 10-4   **Diagram 10-5**

A. He can cross the lane around the "wall" formed by (4) and (3).

B. He can cut to the near low post area and pop out of a downscreen set by (5).

Whichever way (1) chooses to go, (3) will always go opposite. The result will be a double downscreen to initiate the inside triangle. Diagram 10-6 shows Option A with (1) going around the double screen and (3) going opposite (1) to receive (5)'s downscreen.

Diagram 10-7 shows (1) using (5)'s downscreen and (3) going opposite by using (4)'s downscreen.

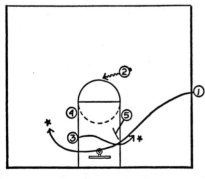
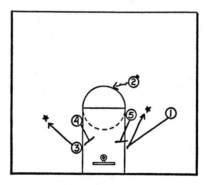

Diagram 10-6   **Diagram 10-7**

Out-of-Bounds Underneath

Again, (1) takes the ball out and the others line up in the box formation. This time, the two biggest players, (4) and (5), are on the blocks and (2) and (3) are high. See Diagram 10-8.

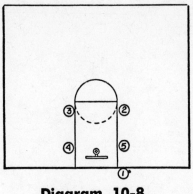

Diagram 10-8

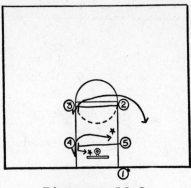

Diagram 10-9

From here, either of two plays may be initiated by (5), the inside man closest to (1). They are: (A) the screen-away and (B) the back-out play.

Play #1: Underneath—(5) Screens Away

(5) calls the play by moving across the lane and screening for (4) who cuts to the ball side. (5) then rolls inside, looking for a possible pass from (1). At the same time, (2) screens for (3) who cuts to the ballside corner. See Diagram 10-9.

(1) looks first for the screen-and-roll play of (5) and (4), and then passes to (3) moving to the ballside corner. (3) then passes to (2) at the head of the key and moves into the lane to form a double screen "wall" with (4). See Diagram 10-10.

(1) can go either way and again (4) will go opposite him.

A. (1) may go around the double screen of (3) and (4) after a change-of-directions move. See Diagram 10-11.

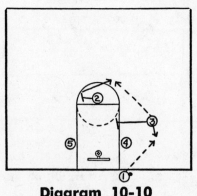

Diagram 10-10

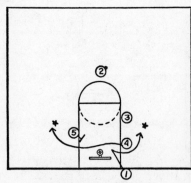

Diagram 10-11

Note that in Diagram 10-11 (4) went opposite (1) and around (5)'s downscreen.

B. (1) may go around (5) and (4) will pop out of (3)'s downscreen. See Diagrams 10-12 and 10-13.

In either case, the inside triangle has been initiated.

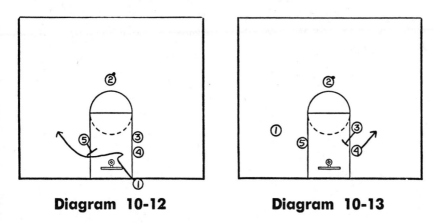

Diagram 10-12   **Diagram 10-13**

Play #2: Underneath—(5) Backs Out to Corner

This play is run from the same formation as the previous play and (5) again initiates the play. This time he backs out to the ballside corner, (4) then screens high for (3), who may cut into the lane or out and (4) always rolls opposite him. See Diagram 10-14.

Note in Diagram 10-15 that (2) moved across the lane to screen.

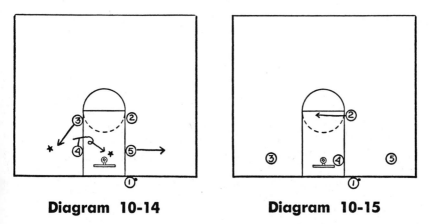

Diagram 10-14   **Diagram 10-15**

(1) looks first at (4) and (3)'s screen-and-roll play and if they are not open, passes to (5) in the corner. By then, (2) cuts back toward the ballside head of the key and receives a pass from (5). See Diagram 10-16.

(5) then forms a double screen "wall" with (4), and (1) can: (A) use the double screen with (4) going opposite (see Diagram 10-17) or (B) (1) may cut around (3) with (4) going opposite by using (5)'s downscreen to pop out. See Diagram 10-18.

In either case, the inside triangle may be run. All of these out-of-bounds plays may be run against man-to-man or zone defenses.

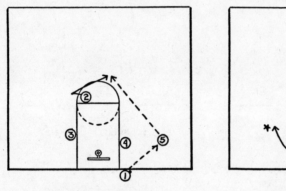

Diagram 10-16

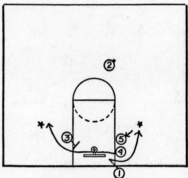

Diagram 10-17

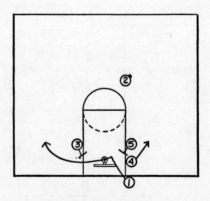

Diagram 10-18

STALL PLAYS

The Stack Stall

This stall is run from the same basic set as the weakside offense. (1) makes his dribble entry and (2) slashes through. However, (1) does not pick up his dribble; instead he continues to dribble. In Diagram 10-19, he dribbles back out front and then to the other wing.

Once (1) picks up his dribble, the inside man on his side (4) must pop out and help him. See (4) in Diagram 10-20.

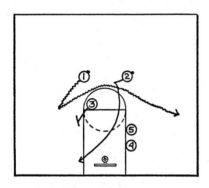

Diagram 10-19   **Diagram 10-20**

(4) and (1) then switch jobs with (1) stacking inside (5) and (4) doing the dribbling. See Diagram 10-21.

In the event the dribbler ((4) in the previous diagram) was forced to pick up his dribble and the man who popped out was being denied

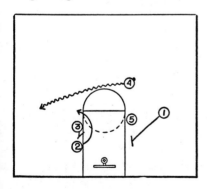
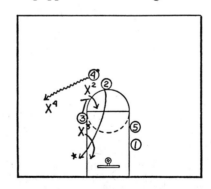

Diagram 10-21   **Diagram 10-22**

the pass, (3) must help. He does this by screening (2)'s man as (2) cuts to the basket. See Diagram 10-22.

This screen does two things: (A) It creates a possible scoring option with (2) getting a lay-up shot, and (B) if (3) forces a switch but (2) is not open, (3) should be open for a pass from (4). See Diagram 10-23.

(3) then does the dribbling and (4) and (2) stack. See Diagram 10-24.

Within the context of this motion, two set plays are run.

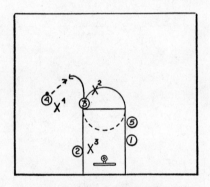

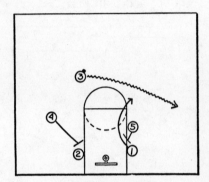

Diagram 10-23   **Diagram 10-24**

The Cross Play

At times, the defender on the man popping out (X2 in Diagram 10-25) makes an extreme overplay. This tells the offside high man to call for a pass from the dribbler, catch it, and quickly look for (2) inside.

The pass from (3) to (2) should be a jump-shot type pass.

The Screen-and-Roll Play

At times, the high man ((3) in Diagram 10-26) will step out and screen for the dribbler ((4)). This tells the inside man on that side to clear to the corner.

(4) then dribbles off (3), and (3) rolls after screening on the other side. (5) screens down for (2) who pops out to the offside head of the key. See Diagram 10-27.

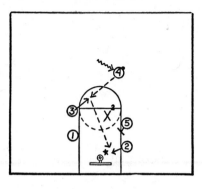

Diagram 10-25

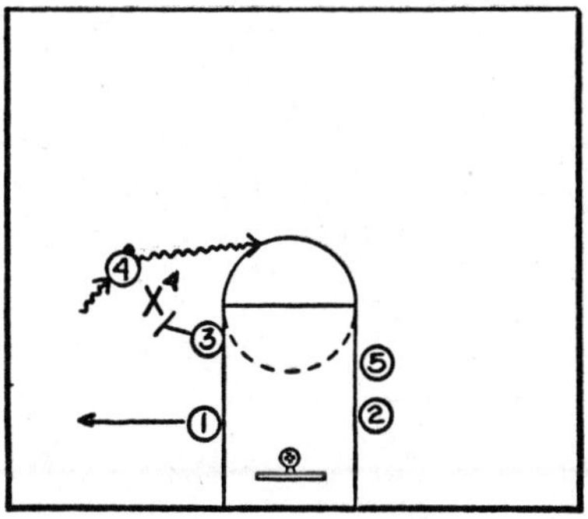

Diagram 10-26

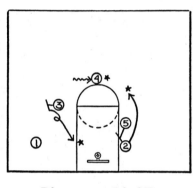

Diagram 10-27

Diagram 10-28

In the right situation, (4) can shoot, or pass to (3) as he rolls to the basket. If neither option is open, he passes to (2). (4) then stacks with (5) as (1) and (3) stack. See Diagram 10-28.

(2) then takes over the dribbling assignment. See Diagram 10-29.

During the basic movement of this stall, common sense must prevail. At all times the best dribblers must be in the inside positions of the stack.

The Wide Stack

It is possible to run this motion with the stackers in a very wide alignment as shown in Diagram 10-30.

This creates a dilemma for the defenders on the inside men (X2 in Diagrams 9-30 and 9-31). If X2 plays between (2) and the basket, he

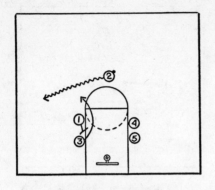

Diagram 10-29

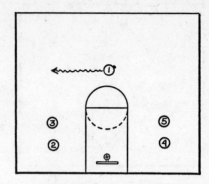

Diagram 10-30

will be vulnerable to (3)'s downscreen and the stall will work. (See Diagram 10-31.)

If he overplays (2), it makes him very vulnerable to the cross play. See Diagram 9-32.

The wide alignment takes away any possible help from X4.

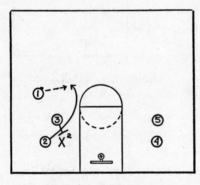

Diagram 10-31

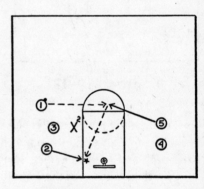

Diagram 10-32

PLAY AT THE FREE THROW LINE

Offensive Free Throw

When our team is shooting a free throw, we want to make it, but if we miss, we want a chance at a second shot, and to be sure the opposition does not get a fast break.

To make it:

1. We shoot 50 free throws each practice.
2. We use proper free throw fundamentals.

   A. Take the ball from the referee and place your feet at the free throw line.

   B. Take a deep breath.

   C. Follow your practice routine in terms of bouncing the ball or any other idiosyncrasies.

   D. Concentrate on the rim and shoot the ball to a pictured spot over it.

   E. Point your shooting elbow and shoot emphasizing the follow-through and being sure not to pull away.

   F. If you make it, check your feet and stay where you are; but if you miss it and have a second shot coming, start the routine over.

   G. Shoot ten mental free throws each day and picture each "swishing" through the basket.

Alignment

In case we miss we use the following alignment. See Diagram 10-33.

On the Shot: We want our biggest man ((5)) to be on the side of their weakest inside man. Our second biggest man ((4)) takes the other second slot. Our third man in the lane ((2)) watches and tries to line up next to our man if they keep only three men in the lane. If they keep four men in the lane, he lines up next to their man assigned to block out the shooter. He then tries to slide down the lane for a possible high rebound to the outside. See Diagram 10-34. Our smallest man is our primary defender and must be our first man back.

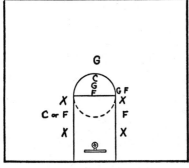

Diagram 10-33

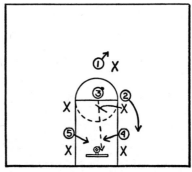

Diagram 10-34

Our second slot players may at times fake and get the blockout man to overcommit. They then can move to the outside. When they get the ball, we beat them down the court.

We want the people at the line to:

1. Get their elbows up high and wide.
2. Crowd the inside of the hash mark.
3. Keep their feet close together.
4. Watch the ball in flight.
5. As soon as the rules permit, take a strong step with the foot closest to the basket and a quick step with the other. Try to get as close to the basket as possible in order to get a tip or rebound, and keep the ball alive.

Defensive Free Throw

Alignment

1. Our big man, (5), must be on the side of their strongest rebounder.
2. Our biggest forward, (4), takes the other inside position and must make an active blockout.
3. Our small forward, (3), plays on our big forward's side and must fight to get a position in the middle.
4. The biggest guard, (2), must actively block out the shooter.
5. Our small guard plays at the head of the key and takes the outlet pass on either side. See Diagram 10-35.

On the Shot:

1. On a defensive free throw, we play close to our high-side hash mark.
2. Our feet are close together and our elbows are wide and high.
3. We watch the ball in flight.
4. Extend the high leg and arm into the lane and make contact.
5. Resist all pressure actively.
6. Leap into the ball and get the outlet pass to (1).
7. Fill a lane.

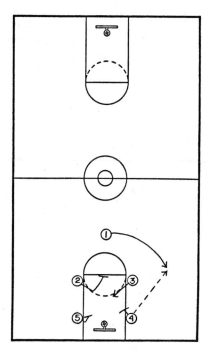

Diagram 10-35

Performing the defensive free throw play correctly is a must. If the offense gets missed shots, they are in position to score and/or get fouled. It should not happen.

SHORT TIME PLAYS

The Last-Second Offensive Play

When a last shot is needed, it is not wise to call time out, make up a new play, and expect your team to run it flawlessly. The last-second shot should be predetermined, practiced, and based on the percentage idea that the best shooter should get the shot with enough time to allow your team to tip it in, if he misses. The opposition should not have time to rebound it and score. Six seconds is the recommended time to take the shot. The following play may be run versus zone or man-to-man defenses.

As (1) makes his dribble entry, (2), the best shooter, cuts through to the low post area. If (2)'s strength lies in the post area, (1) attempts to get the ball to him. See Diagram 10-36.

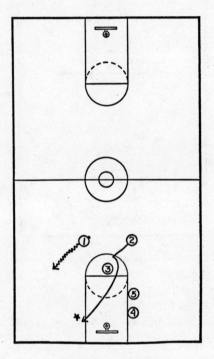

Diagram 10-36

(3) then steps out and takes a pass from (1). (2) may now go either way. He may cut around (5) and (4)'s double screen as shown in Diagram 10-37.

Or he may use (1)'s downscreen. See Diagram 10-38.

As insurance, (4) will always go opposite (2) and use the downscreen on that side.

This play is nothing new to a team running the tilted 2-1-2 offense. It is the heart of the offense. But it is also a play that has been run numerous times by your team and is your best chance to get that winning basket.

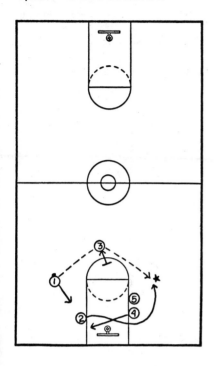

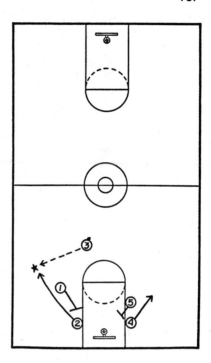

Diagram 10-37   **Diagram 10-38**

Sideline Short Time Play

    With ten seconds on the clock and the opposition playing man-to-man, the team takes the ball out in the back court on the sideline. They line up with (1) taking the ball out and (3) in an apparent guard position; (2) lines up in the back court on (3)'s side, and (5) and (4) are stacked on the ball side. See Diagram 10-39.

    The play starts as (4) pops out of (5)'s downscreen toward the sideline. At the same time, (2) moves up and blindscreens X3 to free (3) for a possible long pass down court. See Diagram 10-40.

    The screen by (2) usually leads to a switch by his defender, X2, and leaves him open for the inbounds pass. As soon as the ball is passed to (2), (5) and (3) move toward the ball. The difficult move is for (1) to cross behind (2) without his man doubling up on (2). See Diagram 10-4.

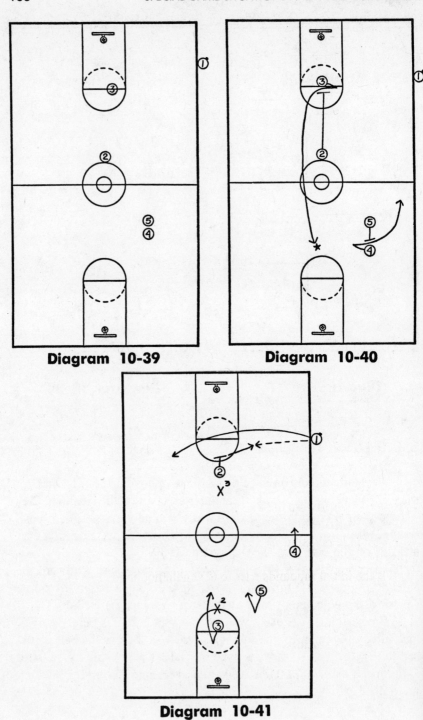

Diagram 10-39

Diagram 10-40

Diagram 10-41

(2) then passes to (5) and the strongside offense is run.

Pass to (5): If (2) passes to (5), (4) backdoors his man; (2) and (1) crisscross off (3). See Diagram 10-42.

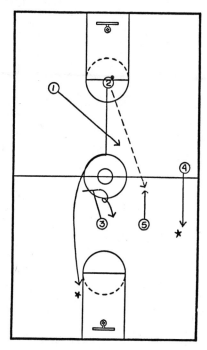

Diagram 10-42

(5) pivots toward the basket and if neither (2) nor (4) are open, (5) turns and hands off to (1) who takes the desperation shot or sets up the offense. This decision by (1) will be determined by the time on the clock.

If the initial inbounds pass to (2) could not be made, (1) may pass to (5), breaking to the ball, and practically the same options are open. See Diagrams 10-43 and 10-44.

Jump Ball Situations

This phase of the game of basketball is an area in transition and may soon be eliminated.

The major objective in a jump ball situation is to obtain the ball.

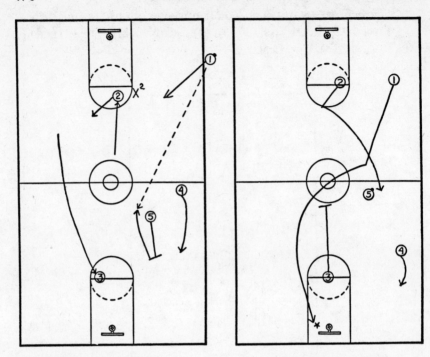

Diagram 10-43   **Diagram 10-44**

The best way to attain this goal is to tip to the open spot. This can be accomplished by giving your guards the dual responsibility of (A) creating the open spot, and (B) being responsible for defensive ball.

In Diagram 10-45, guard (1) creates the open spot against a diamond formation by waiting until both teams line up and then assuming a position that puts two of our players between two of theirs. Guard (2) can line up where he wishes, but is still expected to be our first man back on defense.

(1) and (4) then block out as if they were attempting to keep someone from rebounding.

Diagram 10-46 shows the same method used against a box formation. These special game situations are very important and must be part of the daily practice plan. Many of those presented in this chapter are easy to teach because they are related to the stack offense. This also provides for a smooth transition from the special situation to the basic offense.

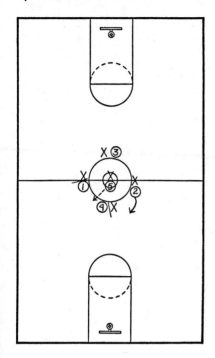

Diagram 10-45

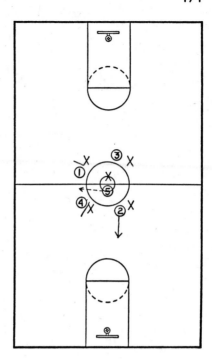

Diagram 10-46

Final Comments

Now that you have looked through the plays in this book, you must ask yourself the following questions.

Have I found a maneuver that I would like to add to my offensive plan? If so, how can I do this in the context of the personnel I have available, and within the framework of the fundamentals of man-to-man offense? Here are some suggestions.

MAINTAINING DEFENSIVE BALANCE

If you desire to run a set play type offense or a limited continuity (where players are specialists and stay in certain areas of the court), your problem is not so great. The outside guard or the offside wing man may be given the primary defensive balance responsibility. However, when you run an interchangeable continuity, much time must be spent to teach the team members that when they are the player who is offside (away from the ball) and high (nearest to midcourt), they are the back man. This can only be accomplished by taking the time in practice to emphasize it.

173

OBTAINING REBOUNDING POSITION

Again, motion is important. If the big man or big men stay inside and have no defensive responsibilities, they should be expected to be the primary rebounders. If, however, you are using a lot of movement, the players must charge the boards with a passion when they are not responsible for defensive balance.

GETTING HIGH PERCENTAGE SHOTS

If your offense is built around stack plays, many high percentage shots can be expected. The two shots that will occur most often are the jump shot from inside the free-throw line extended (12- to 15-foot range) and a one-on-one post-up play. Most players are very adept in these areas and this will increase your field goal percentage. It is wise to utilize a shooting drill in practice that features both of these shots.

ADAPTING TO ZONE DEFENSES

Each of the three offensive sets shown in this book are easily adapted to be used against zone defenses. Chapter Three, Chapter Six, and Chapter Nine show how this may be done. You, the coach, must look at these ideas, analyze the shots they provide, their set, the amount of motion they require, and then decide if they fit your person-nel. I would also suggest that you consider the four-phase plan in Chapter Two. This includes:

(A) Having a simple zone play.
(B) Being able to adapt your man-to-man offense to be used against zones.
(C) Making sure your players are well-versed in individual zone fundamentals.
(D) Having some tempo-changing devices at your disposal.

MEETING DEFENSIVE PRESSURE

This book anticipates defensive pressure and offers methods to meet it. Chapter Ten provides methods that allow you to defeat full and half-court pressure. Each of the three offensive sets provide pressure-relieving devices such as backdoor plays and dribble chases. Also provided are methods of initiating the plays versus pressure and helping man-to-man defenses. Again, you must find those that fit your personnel and coaching philosophy and devise methods of teaching them to your team.

TAKING ADVANTAGE OF DEFENSIVE MATCH-UPS

The basic idea of the stack play is to force a switch and take advantage of defensive mismatches. Along with this, methods are provided that will allow you to take their strong defensive big man away from the basket, wear out the big, slow team with motion, or go inside against the small team.

HAVING DISCIPLINED FLEXIBILITY

This may be the toughest part of coaching offensive basketball. How do I allow my players to do what they are best at without running wild and destroying the continuity and teamwork nature of our game plan? I think it takes some selling of your techniques to your players. You should use the fundamentals of team offense as your tool. Walk through each of your plays and show them why each shot option is functional. Point out the advantage of such things as having someone maintain defensive balance; everyone knowing when it is their turn to charge the boards; attempting to take advantage of mismatches; etc. Show them the point in the play when it is permissible to attempt a one-on-one play, and when it is difficult or impossible. Then break down your offense into drills and work to obtain the proper shot options. However, before you do any of this, make sure you have selected the team techniques that feature the strengths of your personnel and minimize the exposure of their weaknesses.

In conclusion, I would like to emphasize that games are won by players and not plays. Because of this fact, I feel you must spend a lot of time on individual fundamentals, design the plays around the players' skills, and keep them simple. The stack offense is an ideal plan because it is built around a basic core idea (the stack maneuver) that is adaptable to many types of personnel, provides high percentage shots, and is easy to teach.

INDEX